Taylor Swi

Photo courtesy of 13 Management

ISBN 978-1-61774-049-7

HAL•LEONARD®
CORPORATION
7777 W. BLUEMOUND RD. P.O. BOX 13819 MILWAUKEE, WI 53213

Contents

Back to December

Words and Music by
Taylor Swift

Melody:

I'm so glad   you made time to see me.

(Capo 2nd fret)

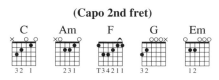

C   Am   F   G   Em

Intro

‖: C |Am   F   :‖

Verse 1

C
I'm so glad you made time to see me.

Am
How's life? Tell me, how is your fam'ly?

F   C   G
I haven't seen them in a while.

C
You've been good, busier than ever.

Am
We small talk, work and the weather.

F   C   G
Your guard is up and I know why.

Pre-Chorus 1

Am   G
Because the last time   you saw me

         C   F
Is still burned in the back of your mind.

           Am   G   F
You gave me roses and I left them there to die.

GUITAR CHORD SONGBOOK

Chorus 1

C
So this is me swallowin' my pride,

        Em   F
Standin' in front of you sayin' I'm sorry for that night.

       C   G
And I go back to December all ___ the time.

      C
It turns out freedom ain't nothin' but missin' you,

Em   F
Wishin' I'd realized what I had when you ___ were mine.

C   G   F
I go back to December, turn ___ around and make it al - right.

    Am   G
I go back to December all ___ the time.

Interlude 1   ‖: C | Am F :‖

Verse 2

C
  These days I haven't been sleepin'.

Am
Stayin' up playin' back myself leavin'.

F   C G
  When your birthday passed and I didn't call.

      C
And I think about summer, all the beautiful times

    Am
I watched you laughin' from the passenger side

    F   C G
And   realized I loved you in the fall.

Pre-Chorus 2

Am   G
  And then the cold came,   the dark days

    C   F
When fear crept into my mind.

      Am   G   F
You gave me all your love and all I gave you was goodbye.

Chorus 2

        C

So this is me swallowin' my pride,

           Em   F

Standin' in front of you sayin' I'm sorry for that night.

           C   G

And I go back to December all ___ the time.

         C

It turns out freedom ain't nothin' but missin' you,

Em   F

Wishin' I'd realized what I had when you ___ were mine.

          C   G   F

I go back to December, turn ___ around and change my own ___ mind.

          Am   G

I go back to December all ___ the time.

Interlude 2   *Repeat Interlude 1*

Bridge

           Am   F

I miss your tan skin, your sweet smile.

        C   G

So good to me, so right.

              Am   F   C

And how you held ___ me in your arms ___ that September night,

            G   Am

The first time you ever saw me cry.

                                  F

Maybe this is wishful thinkin',   probably mindless dreamin',

C   G

   But, if we loved again I swear I'd love you right.

          Am   G   F

I'd go back in time and change ___ it, but I can't.

           Am   G   F

So if the chain is on your door, ___ I under - stand.

Chorus 3

        C
But this is me swallowin' my pride,

            Em   F
Standin' in front of you sayin' I'm sorry for that night.

          C   G
And I go back to December.

      C
It turns out freedom ain't nothin' but missin' you,

Em   F
Wishin' I'd realized what I had when you ___ were mine.

        C   G   F
I go back to December, turn ___ around and make it al - right.

        Am   G   F
I go back to December, turn ___ around and change my own ___ mind.

        Am   G
I go back to December all ___ the time.

Outro | C | Am   F | C |
                                    All the time.

      | Am   F | | ‖

The Best Day

Words and Music by
Taylor Swift

Melody:

I'm five _ years old, _____ it's get - ing

Tune down 1/2 step:
(low to high) Eb-Ab-Db-Gb-Bb-Eb

(Capo 7th fret)

G   Em7   C   D   Dsus4   G5   Em7*   C*   D/F#   Em

Intro

| G | Em7 | C | D | |
| G | Em7 | C | D Dsus4 | |

Verse 1

G5   Em7*
  I'm five years old,

           C*   D
It's getting cold, ____ I've got my big coat on.

G5   Em7*
  I hear your laugh

           C*
And look up smil - ing at you.

  D
I run and run

G5   Em7*
  Past the pumpkin patch

            C*
And the tractor rides.

        D
Look now, the sky is gold.

G5   Em7*
  I hug your legs

           C*   D
And fall asleep ____ on the way home.

Chorus 1

C*   D   G5   D/F♯ Em
I don't know ___ why all the trees ___ change in the fall.

C*   D   G5 D/F♯ Em
I know you're ___ not scared of anything ___ at all.

C*   D   G5 D/F♯
Don't know if Snow ___ White's house is near ___ or far away,

Em   C*   D5
But I know I had the best ___ day with you ___ today.

Interlude | G5 | Em7* | C* | D |

Verse 2

G5   Em7*
I'm thirteen now

         C*   D
And don't know how ___ my friends could be so mean.

G5   Em7*
I come home cry - ing

       C*   D
And you hold ___ me tight and grab the keys.

G5   Em7*
And we drive and drive

       C*   D
Until we found ___ a town far e - nough away,

G5   Em7*
And we talk and win - dow shop

     C*   D
'Till I've ___ forgotten all their names.

Chorus 2

C*   D   G5   D/F♯   Em
I don't know ___ who I'm gonna talk ___ to now at school,

C*   D   G5   D/F♯   Em
But I know I'm laugh - ing on the car ___ ride home with you.

C*   D   G5   D/F♯
Don't know how long ___ it's gonna take ___ to feel ___ okay,

Em   C*   D   G5
But I know I had the best ___ day with you ___ today.

Bridge

C
I have an excellent father.

Em
His strength is making me stronger.

C
God smiles on my little brother.

Em   D
Inside and out, he's bet - ter than I am.

C   G
I grew up in a pretty house

           D/F♯
And I had space ___ to run.

   C   Dsus4   D   Dsus4
And I had the best ___ days with you.

Verse 3

G5   Em7*
  There is a vid - eo

       C   D
I found ____ from back when I was three.

G5   Em7*
  You set up a paint ____ set

       C   D
In the kit - chen and you're talking to me.

G5   Em7*
  It's the age of prin - cesses

        C   D
And pi - rate ships and the Seven Dwarfs.

G5   Em7*
  And Daddy's smart and you're ____ the prettiest

C   D5
La - dy in the whole wide world.

Chorus 3

C   D   G5   D/F♯ Em
  And now I know ____ why all the trees ____ change in the fall.

C   D   G5   D/F♯   Em
  I know you were on ____ my side even when I ____ was wrong.

       C   D
And I love you for giving me your eyes,

G5   D/F♯   Em
  Staying back and watch - ing me shine.

      C   D   G5   D/F♯
And   I didn't know if you ____ knew, so I'm tak - ing this chance to say

Em   C   D   G
  That I had the best ____ day with you ____ today.

Better Than Revenge

Words and Music by
Taylor Swift

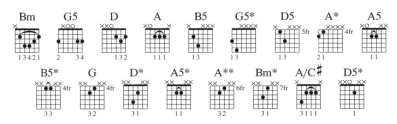

Intro

N.C.

Spoken: Now go stand in the corner and think about what you did.

|Bm |G5 |D |A |

Huh.

|Bm |G5 |D |A |

Huh, ha.   Time for a little revenge.

Verse 1

N.C.(B5)   (G5*)   (D5)

The story starts when it was hot and it was summer and   I had it all.

A*

I had him right there where I wanted him.

Bm   G5

She came along, got him a - lone, and let's hear the applause.

A5   N.C.   A5   N.C.

She took him faster than you could say sabotage.

N.C.(B5)   (G5*)

I never saw it coming, wouldn't have suspected it.

(D5)   (A5)

I underestimated just who I was dealing with.

(B5)   (G5*)

She had to know the pain was beating on me like a drum.

A5   N.C.   A5   N.C.

She underestimated just who she was stealing from.

Chorus 1

Bm   G5
She's not a saint and she's not what you think,

            D   A
She's an actress, whoa.

 Bm   G5
But she's better known for the things that she does

           D   A
On the mattress, whoa.

Bm   G5
Soon she's gonna find stealing other people's toys

        A   G5
On the playground won't make you many friends.

Bm   G5
She should keep in mind, she should keep in mind

           A5
There is nothing I do better than revenge. *(Revenge.) Ha!*

Interlude | Bm | G5 | D | A |

Verse 2

B5*   G
She looks at life like it's a party and she's on the list.

D*   A5*   A**
She looks at me like I'm a trend and *she's so over it.*

Bm*   G
I think her ever-present frown is a little troubling,

   A5   N.C.   A5   N.C.
And   she think's I'm psycho 'cause I like to rhyme her name with things.

B5   G5*
But sophistication isn't what you wear or who you know

D5   A5
Or pushing people down to get you where you wanna go.

B5   G5*
They didn't teach you that in prep school, so it's up to me,

A5   N.C.   A5   N.C.
That no amount of vintage dresses gives you dignity.

(Think about what you did.) Yeah!

Chorus 2

Bm   G5
She's not a saint and she's not what you think,

       D   A
She's an actress, whoa.

  Bm   G5
But she's better known for the things that she does

      D   A
On the mattress, whoa.

Bm   G5
Soon she's gonna find stealing other people's toys

     A   G5
On the playground won't make you many friends.

Bm   G5
She should keep in mind, she should keep in mind

          A5   G5
There is nothing I do better than revenge.

Bridge

   A5   Bm
I'm just another thing for you to roll your eyes at, honey.

  G5   D   A/C♯
You might have him, but haven't you heard?

  Bm   G5
I'm just another thing for you to roll your eyes at, honey.

  D5*   A5
You might have him, but I always get the last…

Guitar Solo

Bm	G5	D	A	
Word,	oo, word,		whoa.	

Bm	G5	D	A	

Chorus 3

Bm   N.C.   G5   N.C.
She's not a saint and she's not   what you think,

       D   A
She's an actress, whoa.

Bm   G5
She's better known for the things that she does

       D   A
On the mattress, whoa.

Bm   G5
Soon she's gonna find stealing other people's toys

       A   G5
On the playground won't make you many friends.

Bm   G5
She should keep in mind, she should keep in mind

        A5
There is nothing I do better than revenge.

Outro

       Bm   G5
Uh, do you still feel like you   know what you're doin'?

      D   A
'Cause I don't think you do.

       Bm   G5
Oh, do you still feel like you   know what you're doin'?

    D   A
I don't think you do, I don't think you do.

          Bm
Let's hear the applause.

       G5   D
Come on, show me how much better you are.

A   Bm   G5
   See, you deserve some applause ____ 'cause you're so much better.

D   N.C.   A5   N.C.
   She took him faster than you could say sabotage.

Breathe

Words and Music by
Taylor Swift and Colbie Caillat

Melody:

I see your face in my mind

Tune down 1/2 step:
(low to high) Eb-Ab-Db-Gb-Bb-Eb

(Capo 7th fret)

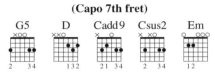

G5   D   Cadd9   Csus2   Em

Intro
‖: G5 D |Cadd9 :‖

Verse 1

       G5   D   Cadd9
I see your face in my mind as I drive away,

         G5   D   Cadd9
'Cause none of us thought it was gonna end that ____ way.

G5   D   Cadd9
People are people and some - times we change our ____ minds,

      G5   D   Cadd9
But it's killing me to see you go ____ after all this ____ time.

Interlude

G5   D   Cadd9
Mm, mm, mm, mm, mm, mm.

G5   D   Cadd9
Mm, mm, mm, mm, mm, mm.

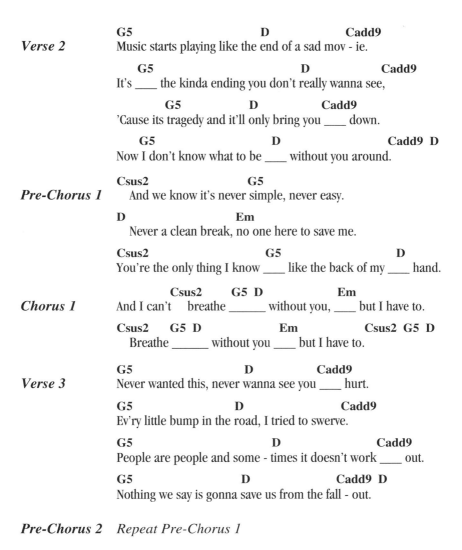

Verse 2

G5   D   Cadd9
Music starts playing like the end of a sad mov - ie.

       G5   D   Cadd9
It's ___ the kinda ending you don't really wanna see,

        G5   D   Cadd9
'Cause its tragedy and it'll only bring you ___ down.

      G5   D   Cadd9 D
Now I don't know what to be ___ without you around.

Pre-Chorus 1

Csus2   G5
And we know it's never simple, never easy.

D   Em
Never a clean break, no one here to save me.

Csus2   G5   D
You're the only thing I know ___ like the back of my ___ hand.

Chorus 1

         Csus2   G5 D   Em
And I can't   breathe _____ without you, ___ but I have to.

Csus2   G5 D   Em   Csus2 G5 D
Breathe _____ without you ___ but I have to.

Verse 3

G5   D   Cadd9
Never wanted this, never wanna see you ___ hurt.

G5   D   Cadd9
Ev'ry little bump in the road, I tried to swerve.

G5   D   Cadd9
People are people and some - times it doesn't work ___ out.

G5   D   Cadd9 D
Nothing we say is gonna save us from the fall - out.

Pre-Chorus 2   *Repeat Pre-Chorus 1*

Chorus 2

       Csus2   G5 D   Em
And I can't   breathe _____ without you, ___ but I have to.

Csus2   G5 D   Em   Csus2 G5 D Em
 Breathe _____ without you ___ but I have to.

|Csus2 G5 |D |

Bridge

      Em   Cadd9
It's two a.m., feeling like I just lost a friend.

              G5   D
Hope you know it's not easy, easy for me.

      Em   Cadd9
It's two a.m., feeling like I just lost a friend.

              G5   D
Hope you know this ain't easy, easy for me.

Pre-Chorus 3

C   G5
 And we know it's never simple, never easy.

D5   Em   C   G5 D5
 Never a clean break, no one here to save ___ me,   oh.

Chorus 3

       Csus2   G5 D   Em
I can't   breathe _____ without you, ___ but I have to.

Csus2   G5 D   Em
 Breathe _____ without you ___ but I have to.

Csus2   G5 D   Em   Csus2 G5 D
 Breathe _____ without you ___ but I have to.

Outro

Csus2   G5   D   Em
    Oo, _____   yeah,   yeah.
  (I'm sorry,   I'm sorry,   I'm sorry,   I'm sorry.)

Csus2   G5   D   Csus2
           Oo. __
  (I'm sorry,   I'm sorry,   I'm sorry,)

Change

Words and Music by
Taylor Swift

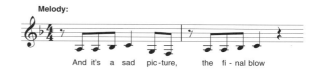

Melody:

And it's a sad pic-ture, the fi-nal blow

Tune down 1 step:
(low to high) D-G-C-F-A-D

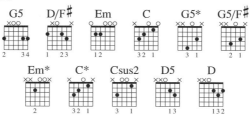

G5 D/F# Em C G5* G5/F#

Em* C* Csus2 D5 D

Intro

‖: G5 | D/F# | Em | C :‖

Verse 1

G5*   G5/F#
And it's a sad picture,   the final blow hits you,

Em*   C*   Csus2
Somebody else gets what you wanted again.

G5*   G5/F#
You know it's all the same,   another time and place,

Em*   C*
Repeating history and you're getting sick of it.

   Em   C   D5
But I believe in whatever you do,

            C   D5
And I'll do anything to see it through

N.C.
Because these things will change.

Chorus 1

G5   D/F#
Can you feel it now?

                      Em   C
These walls that they put ___ up to hold us back will fall ___ down.

        G5   D/F#   Em
This revolu - tion, the time will come ___ for us to finally win.

C   G5
And we'll sing hallelu - jah,

D/F#   Em   C   G5
We'll sing hallelu - jah, ___ oh.

Verse 2

G5*   G5/F#   Em*
So we've been out numbered,   raided and now cornered.

                    C*   Csus2
It's hard to fight when the fight ain't fair.

G5*   G5/F#
We're getting stronger now,   find things they never found.

Em   C   D5
They might be bigger, but we're faster and never scared.

Em   C   D5
You can walk away, ___ say we don't need ___ this.

                    C   D5
But there's something in your eyes says we can beat ___ this

N.C.
'Cause these things will change.

Chorus 2

G5   D/F#
Can you feel it now?

                      Em   C
These walls that they put ___ up to hold us back will fall ___ down.

        G5   D/F#   Em
It's the revolu - tion, the time will come ___ for us to finally win.

C   G5
And we'll sing hallelu - jah,

D/F#   Em   C
We'll sing hallelu - jah, ___ oh.

Guitar Solo ‖: **Em**　| **C**　| **G5**　| **D**　:‖

G5　　　　　　　　**Csus2**　　　　　　　**Em**
Bridge　　Tonight we'll stand, ＿＿ get off our knees,

　　　　　　　　　　　　　　Csus2　　　　　　　　**G5**
　　Fight for what we worked ＿＿ for all these years.

　　　　　　　　　　　　Csus2　　　　　　　　　**Em**
　　And the battle was long, ＿＿ it's the fight of our lives,

　　　　　　　　　　Csus2
　　But we'll stand up champions tonight.

　　It was the night things changed.

G5　　　　　　　　　**D/F♯**
Chorus 3　　Can you see it now?

　　　　　　　　　　　　　Em　　　　　　　　　　**N.C.**
　　These walls that they put ＿＿ up to hold us back fell ＿＿ down.

　　　　　　G5　　　　　　　　　**D/F♯**　　　　　　**Em**
　　It's a revolu - tion, throw your hands up　'cause we never gave ＿＿ in.

C　　　　　　　　　**G5**　**D/F♯**　　　　　**Em** **C**
　　And we'll sing hallelu - jah, ＿＿ we sang hallelu - jah,

　　　　G5 **D/F♯** **Em** **C**
Hallelu - jah.　　　　　Yeah.

Outro　　‖: **G5**　| **D/F♯**　| **Em**　| **C**　:‖ *Play 4 times*

Cold as You

Words and Music by
Taylor Swift and Liz Rose

(Capo 1st fret)

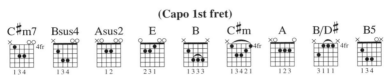

Intro

‖: C#m7 Bsus4 | Asus2   :‖

Verse 1

    E   B   C#m   A
You have a way of coming easily to me.

    E   B/D#   C#m   A
And when you take, you take the very best of me.

    Asus2   B5
So I start a fight 'cause I need to feel something,

           Asus2
And you do what you want 'cause I'm not what you wanted.

Chorus 1

    E   Bsus4
Oh, what a shame.

           C#m7   Asus2
What a rainy ending given to a perfect day.

    E   Bsus4
Just walk away,

          C#m7   Asus2
Ain't no use defending words that you will never say.

    C#m7   Bsus4
And now that I'm sitting here thinking it through,

    Asus2   Bsus4 C#m7 Bsus4 Asus2
I've never been anywhere cold as you.

| C#m7 Bsus4 | Asus2 |

Verse 2

<pre>
         E   Bsus4   C#m7   Asus2
         You put up walls and paint them all a shade of gray.

         E   Bsus4   C#m7   Asus2
         And I stood there loving you and wished ___ them all away.

                         Bsus4
         And you come away with a great little story

             Asus2
         Of a mess of a dreamer with the nerve to adore you.
</pre>

Chorus 2   *Repeat Chorus 1*

Bridge
<pre>
         C#m7   Bsus4
         You never did give a damn ___ thing, honey,

             Asus2   Bsus4
         But I cried, cried for ___ you.

             C#m7   Bsus4
         And I know you wouldn't have told ___ nobody

             Asus2   Bsus4   Asus2
         If I died, died for you, ___ died for ___ you.
</pre>

Chorus 3
<pre>
         E   B/D#
         Oh, what a shame.

                         C#m   Asus2
         What a rainy ending given to a perfect ___ day.

             E   Bsus4
         Oh,   ev'ry smile you fake ___ is so condescending,

         C#m7   Asus2
         Counting all the scars you've made.

             C#m7   Bsus4
         And now that I'm sitting here thinking it through,

             Asus2   Bsus4 C#m7 Bsus4
         I've never been anywhere cold as you.

         Asus2 C#m7 Bsus4 Asus2
         Oo, oh.
</pre>

Crazier

from HANNAH MONTANA: THE MOVIE

Words and Music by
Taylor Swift and Robert Ellis Orrall

Melody:

I'd nev - er gone _ with the wind, _

(Capo 2nd fret)

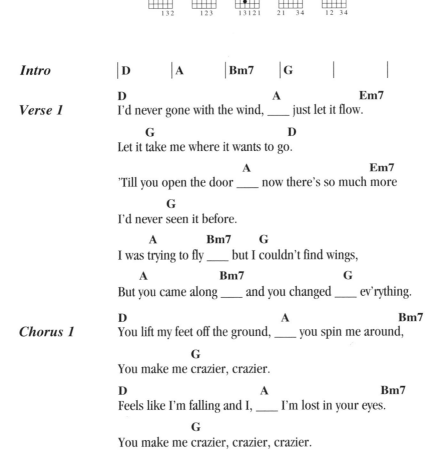

D   A   Bm7   G   Em7

Intro

| D | A | Bm7 | G | | |

Verse 1

      D   A   Em7
I'd never gone with the wind, ____ just let it flow.

         G   D
Let it take me where it wants to go.

                           A   Em7
'Till you open the door ____ now there's so much more

         G
I'd never seen it before.

        A   Bm7   G
I was trying to fly ____ but I couldn't find wings,

        A   Bm7   G
But you came along ____ and you changed ____ ev'rything.

Chorus 1

  D   A   Bm7
You lift my feet off the ground, ____ you spin me around,

                    G
You make me crazier, crazier.

  D   A   Bm7
Feels like I'm falling and I, ____ I'm lost in your eyes.

                    G
You make me crazier, crazier, crazier.

Verse 2

D   A
I've watched from a distance as you,

                    Em7
You've made life your own.

  G   D
Ev'ry sky was your own kind of blue.

                 A   Em7
And I wanted to know ___ how that would feel,

    G
And you made it so real.

A   Bm7   G
You showed me some - thing that I ___ couldn't see,

   A   Bm7   G
You opened my eyes ___ and you made ___ me believe.

Chorus 2

D   A   Bm7
You lift my feet off the ground, ___ you spin me around,

       G
You make me crazier, crazier.

D   A   Bm7
Feels like I'm falling and I, ___ I'm lost in your eyes.

       G
You make me crazier, crazier, crazier. Oh.

Fiddle Solo | D | A | G | |

Bridge

A   Bm7   G
Baby, you showed ___ me what living is for,

  A   Bm7   G
I don't wanna hide ___ any - more.

Chorus 3

D   A   Bm7
You lift my feet off the ground, ___ you spin me around,

       G
You make me crazier, crazier.

D   A   Bm7
Feels like I'm falling and I, ___ I'm lost in your eyes.

       G
You make me crazier, crazier, crazier, crazier, crazier.

Dear John

Words and Music
by Taylor Swift

Long were the nights when my

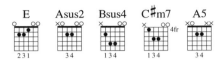

Intro ‖: E | |Asus2 | :‖

Verse 1

E   Asus2
Long were the nights when my days once revolved around you.

E   Asus2
Counting my footsteps, praying the floor won't fall ____ through again.

Pre-Chorus 1

    Bsus4
And my mother accused me

  C#m7   Bsus4
Of los - ing my mind

    Asus2
But I swore ____ I was fine.

Verse 2

    E   Asus2
You paint me a blue sky and go back and turn it to rain.

    E
And I lived in your chess game,

       Asus2
But you changed the rules ev'ry day.

GUITAR CHORD SONGBOOK

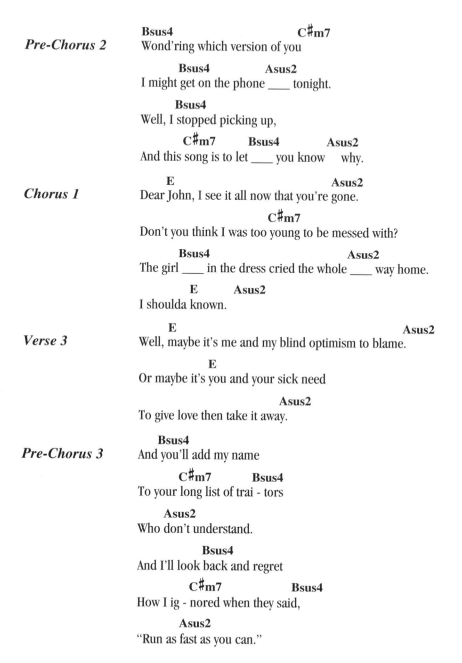

Pre-Chorus 2

Bsus4   C#m7
Wond'ring which version of you

       Bsus4   Asus2
I might get on the phone ___ tonight.

       Bsus4
Well, I stopped picking up,

       C#m7   Bsus4   Asus2
And this song is to let ___ you know   why.

Chorus 1

       E   Asus2
Dear John, I see it all now that you're gone.

               C#m7
Don't you think I was too young to be messed with?

       Bsus4   Asus2
The girl ___ in the dress cried the whole ___ way home.

       E   Asus2
I shoulda known.

Verse 3

       E   Asus2
Well, maybe it's me and my blind optimism to blame.

       E
Or maybe it's you and your sick need

              Asus2
To give love then take it away.

Pre-Chorus 3

       Bsus4
And you'll add my name

       C#m7   Bsus4
To your long list of trai - tors

       Asus2
Who don't understand.

       Bsus4
And I'll look back and regret

       C#m7   Bsus4
How I ig - nored when they said,

       Asus2
"Run as fast as you can."

	E Asus2
Chorus 2	Dear John, I see it all now that you're gone.

                           C#m7
Don't you think I was too young to be messed with?

          Bsus4   Asus2
The girl ____ in the dress cried the whole ____ way home.

        E   Asus2
Dear John, I see it all now, it was wrong.

                        C#m7
Don't you think nineteen's too young to be played

          Bsus4   Asus2
By your dark, ____ twisted games when I loved you so?

A5   E   Asus2
  I shoulda known.

	C#m7 Bsus4
Bridge	You are an expert at sorry, and keeping lines blurry.

Asus2
Never impressed by me acing your tests.

         C#m7   Bsus4
All the girls ____ that you've run dry have tired, lifeless eyes

           Asus2
'Cause you burned them out.

  Bsus4   C#m7   Bsus4
But I took your matches before ____ fire could catch ____ me,

     Asus2
So don't look now.

  Bsus4   Asus2
I'm shining like fireworks over your sad, empty town.

Interlude　　　| E　　　　　|　　　　　|Asus2　　|　　　　　　|

　　　　　　　　　　Yeah, ___ yeah. _____ Oh,

　　　　　　　| C#m7　　| Bsus4　　| Asus2　　|　　　　　　|

　　　　　　　　　　oh.

　　　　　　　　　　　　　　E　　　　　　　　　　　　　　Asus2
Chorus 3　　Dear John, I see it all now that you're gone.

　　　　　　　　　　　　　　　　　　C#m7
　　　　　　　Don't you think I was too young to be messed with?

　　　　　　　　　　　　Bsus4　　　　　　　　　　　　　　Asus2
　　　　　　　The girl ___ in the dress cried the whole ___ way home.

　　　　　　　E　　　　　　　　　　　　　Asus2
　　　　　　　　I see it all now that you're gone.

　　　　　　　　　　　　　　　　　　C#m7
　　　　　　　Don't you think I was too young to be messed with?

　　　　　　　　　　　　Bsus4　　　　　　　　　Asus2
　　　　　　　The girl ___ in the dress wrote you a song.

　　　　　　　　　　　　　　　E　　　　　　　　Asus2
Outro　　　You should've known, you shoulda known.

　　　　　　　E　　　　　　　　　　　　　　Asus2
　　　　　　　　Don't you think I was too young?

　　　　　　　　　　　　　　　　　E
　　　　　　　You shoulda known.

Enchanted

Words and Music by
Taylor Swift

Melody:

There I was a - gain to - night,

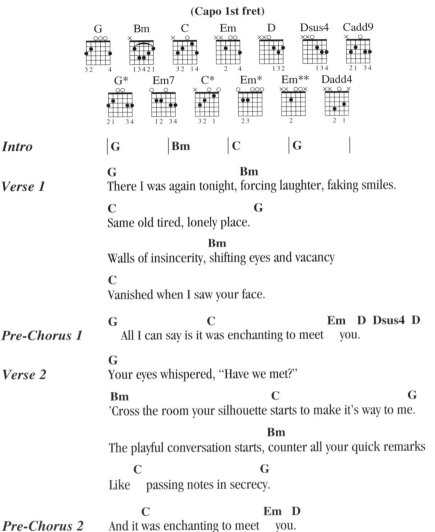

(Capo 1st fret)

G   Bm   C   Em   D   Dsus4   Cadd9

G*   Em7   C*   Em*   Em**   Dadd4

Intro

| G | Bm | C | G | |

Verse 1

G   Bm
There I was again tonight, forcing laughter, faking smiles.

C   G
Same old tired, lonely place.

Bm
Walls of insincerity, shifting eyes and vacancy

C
Vanished when I saw your face.

Pre-Chorus 1

G   C   Em D Dsus4 D
　All I can say is it was enchanting to meet　you.

Verse 2

G
Your eyes whispered, "Have we met?"

Bm   C   G
'Cross the room your silhouette starts to make it's way to me.

Bm
The playful conversation starts, counter all your quick remarks

C   G
Like   passing notes in secrecy.

Pre-Chorus 2

C   Em D
And it was enchanting to meet   you.

C   Em D N.C.
All I can say is I was enchanted to meet   you.

Chorus 1

Cadd9   G*   D   Cadd9
  This night is sparklin' don't you let it go.

        G*   D   Cadd9
I'm wonder - struck, blushing all the way home.

        G* D   Cadd9
I'll spend for - ever wond'rin' if you knew

                Em7 D G*
I was enchanted to meet   you.

Verse 3

      G*   Bm
The ling'ring question kept me up: two A.M., who do you love?

  C*   G*
I   wonder 'till I'm wide awake.

                  Bm
And now I'm pacing back and forth wishing you were at my door.

    C   G*
I'd   open up and you would say,

Pre-Chorus 3

      C*   Em* D Dsus4
"Hey, it was enchanting to meet   you."

  D   C*   Em*   D Dsus4 D N.C.
All I know is I was enchanted to meet   you.

Chorus 2

Cadd9   G*   D   Cadd9
  This night is sparklin' don't you let it go.

        G*   D   Cadd9
I'm wonder - struck, blushing all the way home.

        G* D   Cadd9 Em7 D
I'll spend for - ever wond'rin' if you knew

Cadd9   G*   D   Cadd9
  That this night is flawless, don't you let it go.

        G*   D   Cadd9
I'm wonder - struck, dancin' a - round all alone.

        G* D   Cadd9
I'll stand for - ever wond'rin' if you knew

                Em7 D
I was enchanted to meet   you.

Guitar Solo

| G | Bm | C | G* | |
| | Bm | C* | D | |

                   And this is me prayin' that

Bridge

Cadd9   Em7   D
This was the very first page,   not where the storyline ends.

Cadd9   Em7   D
My thoughts will echo your name   until I see you again.

Cadd9   Em7   D
These are the words I held back   as I was leaving too soon:

C*   Em** Dadd4
I was enchanted to meet   you.

Interlude

G   Bm
(Please don't be in love with someone el, else.)

C   G
(Please don't have somebody waitin' on you.)

G*   Bm
Oh.
(Please don't be in love with someone el, else.)

C   G*
Oh.
(Please don't have somebody waitin' on you.)

Chorus 3

Cadd9   G*   D   Cadd9
This night is sparklin' don't you let it go.

           G*   D   Cadd9
I'm wonder - struck, blushing all the way home.

            G* D   Cadd9 Em7 D
I'll spend for - ever wond'rin' if you knew

Cadd9   G*   D   Cadd9
This night is flawless, don't you let it go.

           G*   D   Cadd9
I'm wonder - struck, dancin' a - round all alone.

           G* D   Cadd9
I'll stand for - ever wond'rin' if you knew

                 Em7 D
I was enchanted to meet   you.

Outro

G*   Bm*
(Please don't be in love with someone el, else.)

C*   G*
(Please don't have somebody waitin' on you.)

Fearless

Words and Music by Taylor Swift,
Liz Rose and Hillary Lindsey

Melody:

There's some-thing 'bout the way

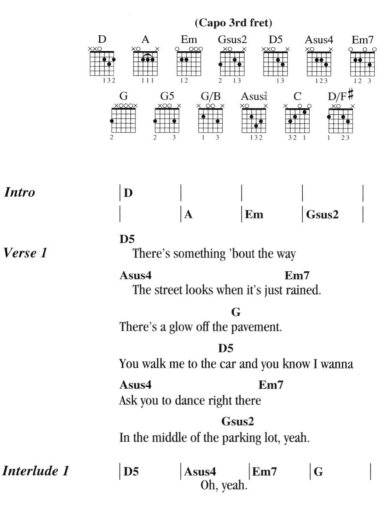

(Capo 3rd fret)

D   A   Em   Gsus2   D5   Asus4   Em7

G   G5   G/B   Asus$\frac{2}{4}$ C   D/F#

Intro
| D | | | | |
| | A | Em | Gsus2 | |

Verse 1

        D5
    There's something 'bout the way

Asus4   **Em7**
   The street looks when it's just rained.

               G
There's a glow off the pavement.

             D5
You walk me to the car and you know I wanna

Asus4   **Em7**
Ask you to dance right there

               Gsus2
In the middle of the parking lot, yeah.

Interlude 1
| D5 | Asus4 | Em7 | G | |

        Oh, yeah.

Verse 2

D5
We're driving down the road,

Asus4   Em7
I wonder if you know ____ I'm trying so hard

G
Not to get caught up now.

D5   Asus4
But you're just so cool, run your hands through your hair,

Em7   G5   Asus4
Absentmindedly makin' me want you.

Chorus 1

D5   A   Em7
And I don't know how it gets better than this.

                  G5   A
You take my hand and drag me headfirst. Fearless.

D5   A   Em7
And I don't know why, but with you I'd dance

          G5   A
In a storm in my best dress. Fearless.

Interlude 2 | D5 | Asus4 | Em7 | G |

Verse 3

D
So, baby, drive slow

Asus4   Em7
'Till we run outta road

             G
In this one horse town.

             D
I wanna stay right here ____ in this passenger seat.

A   Em7
You put your eyes on me.

          Gsus2   Asus4
In this moment now, capture it, re - member it.

Chorus 2

D5   A   Em7
 'Cause I don't know how it gets better than this.

             G5   A
You take my hand and drag me headfirst. Fearless.

D5   A   Em7
 And I don't know why, but with you I'd dance

       G5   A
In a storm in my best dress. Fearless.

Guitar Solo

| Em7 | G5 | D5 | Asus4 G/B |
| Em7 | G5 | D5 | Asus²₄ G/B |

Bridge

C   D5
 Well, you stood there with me ___ in the doorway.

       Em   D/F# G5   Asus4
My hands ___ shake, I'm not usu'lly ___ this way.

    C   D5
But you pull me in and I'm a little more brave.

       Em   D/F# G5   Asus4
It's a first ___ kiss, it's flaw - less, really something. It's fearless.

Interlude 3

| D5 | Asus4 | Em7 | G |
     Oh, ___ yeah. ___

Chorus 3   *Repeat Chorus 2*

Chorus 4   *Repeat Chorus 2*

Outro

D5   A   Em7 G5
 Oh, oh, ___ aw, ___ yeah.

Fifteen

Words and Music by
Taylor Swift

Melody:

You take a deep breath and you walk ___

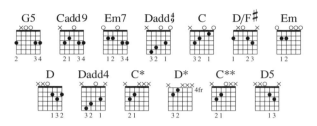

Intro |G5 |Cadd9 |Em7 |Cadd9 |

Verse 1

G5   Cadd9
   You take a deep breath and you walk ___ through the doors,

          Em7   Cadd9
It's the morn - ing of your very first day.

          G5   Cadd9
You say, "Hi," to your friends you ain't seen in a while,

          Em7   Cadd9
Try and stay out of ev'rybody's way.

G5   Cadd9
   It's your freshman year and you're gonna be here

          Em7   Cadd9
For the next ___ four years in this   town.

                    G5   Cadd9
Hoping one of those ___ senior boys will wink at you and say,

          Em7   Cadd9
"You know, I haven't seen you around ___ before."

Chorus 1

G5
'Cause when you're ___ fifteen

Em7   Dadd⁴₃
And   somebody tells you they love ___ you

C
You're gonna believe ___ them.

G5
And when you're ___ fifteen,

D/F#   Em   Cadd9
Feel - ing like there's noth - ing to figure out,

Em   D
Well,   count to ten, take it in,

G5   D/F# Cadd9
This is life before you know who you're gon - na be.

Dadd4
Fifteen.

Interlude | G5 | Cadd9 | Em7 | Cadd9 |

G5   Cadd9
Verse 2   You sit in class next to a red - head named Abigail

Em7   Cadd9
And soon enough you're best friends.

G5   Cadd9
Laughing at the other girls who think they're so cool,

Em7   Cadd9
We'll be out of here as soon as we can.

G5   Cadd9
And then you're on your very first date

Em7   Cadd9
And he's got a car ___ and you're feeling like fly - ing.

G5   Cadd9
And your mama's waiting up, and you're thinking he's the one,

Em7   C*
And you're danc - ing 'round the room when the night   ends,

D*   C**
When the night ___ ends.

Chorus 2

Dadd4   **G5**
'Cause when you're ___ fifteen

    Em7   **Dadd⁴₉**
And   somebody tells you they love ___ you

                   C
You're gonna believe ___ them.

             G5
And when you're ___ fifteen,

    D/F♯   **Em**   **Cadd9**
And ___ your first kiss makes ___ your head spin 'round.

    Em   **D**
But   in your life you'll do things

                G5   **D/F♯**   **Cadd9**
Greater than dating the boy on the foot - ball team.

     Dadd4
I didn't know it at fifteen.

Guitar Solo | **G5** | **Cadd9** | **Em7** | **Cadd9**   **D** |

Bridge

Cadd9   **Em7**   **D5**
When all you want - ed was to be want - ed,

                G5
Wish you could go back and tell yourself

   D/F♯   **Cadd9** **Dadd4**
What you know now.

Verse 3

G5   **Cadd9**
Back then I swore I was gonna mar - ry him someday,

   Em7   **Cadd9**
But I realized some bigger dreams of mine.

   G5   **Cadd9**
And Abigail gave ev'rything ___ she had

     Em7   **C**
To a boy ___ who changed his mind, ___ and we both cried.

Chorus 3

                         G5
'Cause when you're ____ fifteen

      Em7   **Dadd⁴**
And   somebody tells you they love ____ you

                  C
You're gonna believe ____ them.

             G5
And when you're ____ fifteen,

      D/F♯   **Em**   **Cadd9**
Don't ____ forget to look ____ before you fall.

Em   **D**
  I've found time can heal most   anything

                G5   **D/F♯**   **Cadd9**
And you just might find out who you're sup - posed to be.

        Em   **D/F♯**   **Cadd9**
I didn't know who I was s'posed to be

Dadd4
  At fifteen.

Outro | **G5** | **Cadd9** |

Em7   **C**
  La, la, la, la, la, la, ____ la, la, la, la.

G5   **Cadd9**
  La, la, la, la, la, la, ____ la, la, la, la.

Em7
  La, la, la, la, la, la.

Cadd9   **G5**   **Cadd9**
  Your very first ____ day.   Uh, take a deep breath, girl.

Em7   **Cadd9**
  Take a deep breath as you walk ____ through the doors.

Forever & Always

Words and Music by
Taylor Swift

Melody:

Once up - on a time, ___

(Capo 3rd fret)

Cadd9   G5   D   D/A   C   Em   G/B   D5

| | | | | | | | |

Verse 1

              Cadd9   G5   D
Once up - on a time, I be - lieve it was a Tuesday

              Cadd9   G5   D
When I caught your eye and we caught on to something.

              Cadd9   G5   D
I hold on - to the night you looked me in the eye

              Cadd9   D/A
And told me you loved me. ___ Were you just kidding?

              Cadd9   G5   D
'Cause it seems to me this thing is breaking down.

              Cadd9   G5   D
We almost never speak, I don't feel welcome anymore.

              Cadd9   G5
Baby, what happened? Please tell me 'cause one second it was perfect,

              D
Now you're halfway out the door.

Pre-Chorus 1

              C   G5
And I stare at the phone, he still hasn't called

              D   Em
And then you feel so low you can't feel ___ nothing at all.

              C   G/B   D
And you flash back to when he ___ said forever and al - ways.

Chorus 1

              C   G5
Oh, oh, and it rains in your bedroom, ev - 'rything is wrong.

              D   Em
It rains when you're here and it rains ___ when you're gone.

              C   G5   D   N.C.
'Cause I was there when you ___ said forever and al - ways.

Verse 2

      Cadd9   G5   D
Was I out of line? Did I say something way too honest?

        Cadd9   G5   D
Made you run and hide like a scared little boy.

         Cadd9   G5   D
I looked in - to your eyes, thought I knew you for a minute.

       Cadd9   D
Now I'm not so sure.

         Cadd9   N.C.
So here's to ev'rything coming down to nothing.

        Cadd9   G5   D
Here's to silence, that cuts me to the core.

         Cadd9   G5   D
Where is this going? Thought I knew for a minute,

      Cadd9   D
But I don't anymore.

Pre-Chorus 2

           C   G5
And I stare at the phone, he still hasn't called

          D   Em
And then you feel so low you can't feel ___ nothing at all.

        C   G5   D
And you flash back to when he ___ said forever and al - ways.

Chorus 2

          C   G5
Oh, oh, and it rains in your bedroom, ev - 'rything is wrong.

  D   Em
It rains when you're here and it rains ___ when you're gone.

        C   G5   D
'Cause I was there when you ___ said forever and al - ways.

You didn't mean it, baby.

Interlude | Em   D C | | Em   D C | |
                          I don't think so.   Oh, _

        | D |
        ____ ho. ____

Guitar Solo		C		G5		D		Em		
		C		G5		D				

Bridge

       Em   **Cadd9**
Oh, back up, baby, back ___ up.

            D5
Did you for - get ev'rything?

Em   **C**
Back up, baby, back ___ up.

            D5   **Cadd9**
Did you for - get ev'rything?

Chorus 3

D5   **C**   **G5**
  'Cause it rains in your bedroom, ev - 'rything is wrong.

    D   **Em**
It rains when you're here and it rains ___ when you're gone.

     C   **G5**   **D**
'Cause I was there when you ___ said forever and al - ways.

Pre-Chorus 3

         C   **G5**
Oh I stare at the phone, he still hasn't called

         D   **Em**
And then you feel so low you can't feel ___ nothing at all.

      C   **G5**   **D**
And you flash back to when we ___ said forever and al - ways.

Chorus 4

     C   **G5**
And it rains in your bedroom, ev - 'rything is wrong.

    D   **Em**
It rains when you're here and it rains ___ when you're gone.

     C   **G5**   **D**
'Cause I was there when you ___ said forever and al - ways.

You didn't mean it, baby.

Outro

| **Em** | **D** | **C** | | | **Em** | **D** | **C** | ‖
You said forever and al - ways,   yeah.

Haunted

Words and Music by
Taylor Swift

Tune down 1 step:
(low to high) D-G-C-F-A-D

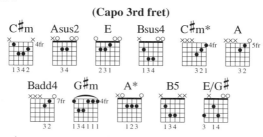

(Capo 3rd fret)

Intro

‖: C#m | Asus2 | E | Bsus4 :‖

Verse 1

C#m*   A
You and I walk a fragile line.

Badd4   C#m*
  I have known it all this time,

                   A   Badd4
But I never thought I'd live to see it break.

C#m*   A
  It's getting dark and it's all too quiet

         Badd4
And I can't trust anything now.

         C#m*   A   Badd4
And it's comin' over you like it's all a big mistake.

Pre-Chorus 1

      C#m   Asus2
  Whoa, holdin' my breath,   won't lose you again.

G#m   A*   B5
Somethin's made your eyes go cold.

Chorus 1

C#m   Asus2   E
Come on, come on, ____ don't leave me like this.

                Bsus4   C#m
I thought I had you figured out.

                      Asus2
Something's gone terribly wrong.

                Bsus4
You're all I wanted.

C#m   Asus2   E
Come on, come on, ____ don't leave me like this.

                Bsus4   C#m
I thought I had you figured out.

                      Asus2
Can't breathe when - ever you're gone.

                Bsus4
Can't turn back, now. I'm haunted.

Interlude 1 |C#m |Asus2 |E |Bsus4 |

Verse 2

C#m   Asus2
Stood there and watched you walk away

Bsus4   C#m
From ev'rything we had,

                 Asus2   Bsus4
But I still mean ev'ry word I said ____ to you.

C#m   Asus2
He will try to take a - way my pain,

Bsus4   C#m
And he just might make me smile.

                  Asus2   Bsus4
But the whole time I'm wishin' he was you ____ instead.

Pre-Chorus 2

C#m   Asus2
Oh, holdin' my breath,   won't see you again.

G#m   A*   B5
Somethin' keeps me holdin' on to nothing.

Chorus 2   *Repeat Chorus 1*

| *Guitar Solo* | | C#m | | Asus2 | | E | | Bsus4 | |

Bridge

      C#m Bsus4 Asus2
I know.

      C#m Bsus4 Asus2
I know.

      C#m Bsus4 Asus2   **Bsus4**
I just know _____ you're not gone.

      E/G#   **Asus2**
You can't ___ be gone, ___ no.

Chorus 3

C#m   **A***   **E**
  Come on, come on, ___ don't leave me like this.

     Bsus4   **C#m**
I thought I had you figured out.

     Asus2
Somethin's gone terribly wrong.

     B5
Won't finish what you started.

C#m   **Asus2**   **E**
  Come on, come on, ___ don't leave me like this.

     Bsus4   **C#m**
I thought I had you figured out.

     Asus2
Can't breathe when - ever you're gone.

Bsus4
Can't go back, I'm haunted.

Interlude 2

C#m   **Asus2**   **E**   **Bsus4**
  Oh, ho, ___ ho, ___ ho.

Outro

C#m
You and I walk a fragile line.

Asus2   **E**
  I have known it all this time.

        Bsus4
Never ever thought I'd see it break.

      C#m
Never thought I'd see it.

Hey Stephen

Words and Music by
Taylor Swift

Tune down 1/2 step:
(low to high) E♭-A♭-D♭-G♭-B♭-E♭

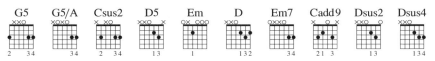

Intro	G5 G5/A Csus2 G5/A G5

            G5   **G5/A** **Csus2**   **G5/A G5**
Intro   Mm, mm, mm, ___ mm, ___ mm, mm, mm.

                                  G5/A   **Csus2**   **G5/A G5**
Mm, mm, mm, ___ mm, ___ mm.

                             G5/A   **Csus2**   **G5/A**   **G5**
Mm, mm, mm, ___ mm, ___ mm, mm, mm, ___ mm.

                          G5/A Csus2 **G5/A G5**
Mm, mm, mm, _____ yeah.

            G5   **G5/A** **Csus2**   **G5/A**
Verse 1   Hey, Ste - phen, I know looks can be deceiv - ing

               G5   **G5/A Csus2** **G5/A G5**
But I know I saw a light in you.

                               G5/A   **Csus2**
And as we walked, ___ we were talking.

                       G5/A Csus2   **G5/A Csus2 G5/A G5**
I did - n't say ___ half the things I want - ed to.

                          G5/A   **Csus2**   **G5/A G5**
Of all the girls ___ toss - ing rocks at your win - dow.

                          G5/A   **Csus2**   **G5/A G5**
I'll be the one ___ wait - ing there even when it's cold.

                     G5/A   **Csus2**   **G5/A**
Hey, Ste - phen, boy, you might have me believ - ing

    G5   **G5/A Csus2**
I don't always have to be alone.

Chorus 1

G5   G5/A Csus2   D5
  'Cause I can't help it if   you look like an angel.

G5   G5/A Csus2
  Can't help it if I wan - na kiss you in the rain.

D5 Em   D
So come feel this magic I've been feeling since I met you.

  G5   Csus2
Can't help it if there's no one else.

    D5 N.C.
Mm, ____ I can't help myself.

Interlude 1

G5 G5/A Csus2 G5/A G5
  Mm, mm, mm.

     G5/A Csus2
Mm, mm, mm, ____ mm, ____ mm, mm, mm.

Verse 2

G5   G5/A Csus2   G5/A
  Hey, Ste - phen, I've been holding back this feel - in'

 G5   G5/A Csus2 G5/A G5
So I've got some things to say to you.   Ha.

     G5/A Csus2
I've seen it all ____ so I thought,

     G5/A G5   G5/A Csus2
But I nev - er seen nobody shine the way you do.

G5   G5/A Csus2   G5/A G5
  The way you walk, way you talk, way you say my name.

     G5/A Csus2   G5/A G5
It's beautiful, ____ won - derful, don't you ev - er change.

     G5/A Csus2   G5/A
Hey, Ste - phen, why are people always leav - ing?

 G5   G5/A Csus2 G5/A G5
I think you and I should stay the same.

Chorus 2

```
G5                        G5/A  Csus2              D5
  'Cause I can't help it if     you look like an angel.

G5              G5/A  Csus2
  Can't help it if I wan - na kiss you in the rain.

D5  Em                        D
So    come feel this magic I've been feeling since I met you.

        G5                          Csus2
Can't help it if there's no one else.

        D
Mm, ____ I can't help myself.
```

Interlude 2

```
G5  G5/A Csus2            G5/A
  Mm, _____ mm, mm, mm.

G5                   G5/A    Csus2
Mm, mm, mm, mm, ___ mm, ___ mm.
```

Bridge

```
Em                        D
  They're dimming the street ____ lights.

          G5
You're perfect for me.

          Csus2
Why aren't you here ____ tonight?

Em7              D
  I'm waiting alone ____ now,

              G5
So come on and come ____ out and pull me

Cadd9           Dsus2
  Near and shine, ____ shine, shine.
```

Verse 3

```
G5          G5/A  Csus2                    G5/A
  Hey Ste - phen, I could give you fifty rea - sons

    G5                  G5/A      Csus2 G5/A G5
Why I should be the one you choose.

          G5/A  Csus2                    G5/A
All those oth - er girls, ____ well, they're beauti - ful,

G5                D5          Cadd9
But would they write a song for you?    *Ha, Ha!*
```

Chorus 3

```
G5                       G5/A Csus2           D5
  'Cause I can't help it if    you look like an angel.

G5                  G5/A  Csus2
  Can't help it if I wan - na kiss you in the rain.

D5  Em                            D
So     come feel this magic I've been feeling since I met you.

  G5                            Csus2
Can't help it if there's no one else.

        D                          G5 G5/A Csus2           Dsus4
Mm, ___ I can't help myself ___  if      you look like an angel.

G5                  G5/A  Csus2
  Can't help it if I wan - na kiss you in the rain.

D5  Em                            D
So     come feel this magic I've been feeling since I met you.

  G5                            Csus2
Can't help it if there's no one else.

     D5  N.C.
Mm, ___ I can't help myself.
```

Outro

```
G5  G5/A  Csus2  G5/A  G5  G5/A  Csus2  G5/A
    Mm,   mm,    my  - self.

G5                  G5/A      Csus2
Mm, mm, mm, mm, ___ mm, ___ mm.

        G5/A  G5              G5/A  Csus2
Can't help my - self. I can't help my - self.

        G5/A  G5
Oh, oh, oh.

              G5/A      Csus2              G5/A       G5
Mm, mm, mm, ___ mm, ___ mm, mm, mm, ___ mm.

              G5/A      Csus2
Mm, mm, mm, ___ mm, ___ mm.

G5           G5/A      Csus2              G5/A       G5
Mm, mm, mm, ___ mm, ___ mm, mm, mm, ___ mm.

              G5/A      Csus2
Mm, mm, mm, ___ mm, ___ mm. Mm, mm.
```

Innocent

Words and Music by
Taylor Swift

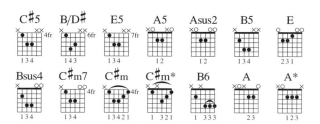

Intro

|C#5 B/D# E5 |A5 | C#5 B/D# E5 |A5 |
(Ah, _____ ah, ah.)

Verse 1

C#5   B/D#   E5   A5
I guess you really did it this time.

C#5   B/D#   E5   Asus2
Left your - self in your war path,

C#5   B/D#   E5   Asus2
Lost your balance on a tight rope,

C#5   B/D#   E5   Asus2
Lost your mind try'n' to get it back.

Pre-Chorus 1

B5   C#5 Asus2
Wasn't it eas - ier ____ in your lunchbox days?

B5   C#5   Asus2
Always a big - ger bed ____ to crawl into.

B5   C#5 Asus2
Wasn't it beau - tiful ____ when you believed in ev'rything,

B5   C#5   Asus2
And ev'rybody believed ____ in you?

Chorus 1

E
It's alright, just wait and see.

    Bsus4
Your   string of lights are still bright to me.

    C#m7
Oh,   who you are is not where you've been.

Asus2
You're still an innocent.

Interlude 1

|**C#5**   **Bsus4**   **E** |**Asus2** |
                                        You're still an innocent.

|**C#5**   **Bsus4**   **E** |**Asus2** |

Verse 2

C#5   **B/D#**   **E5**   **A5**
Did some things ___ you can't speak of,

C#5   **B/D#**   **E5**   **Asus2**
But at night ___ you live it all again.

C#5   **B/D#**   **E5**   **Asus2**
You wouldn't be shattered on the floor now

C#5   **B/D#**   **E5**   **Asus2**
If only you had seen what you know now ___ then.

Pre-Chorus 2

B5   **C#5** **Asus2**
Wasn't it eas - ier ___ in your firefly-catching days

B5   **C#5**   **Asus2**
When ev'rything out ___ of reach

Someone bigger brought down to you?

B5   **C#5** **Asus2**
Wasn't it beau - tiful ___ running wild 'till you fell asleep

B5   **C#5** **A5**
Before the monsters caught up to   you?

Chorus 2

E
It's alright, just wait and see.

Bsus4
Your   string of lights are still bright to me.

C#m7
Oh,   who you are is not where you've been.

Asus2
You're still an innocent.

E
It's okay, ah, life is a tough crowd.

Bsus4
Thirty-two and still growing up now.

C#m7
Who you are is not what you did.

Asus2
You're still an innocent.

Interlude 2

| C#5   Bsus4   E | Asus2 |

Bridge

C#m*
Time turns flames to embers,

B6
You'll have new Septembers.

A
Ev'ryone of us has messed up, too.

C#m7
Oo, minds change like weather.

Bsus4
I hope you'll remember.

A*   Asus2
Today is never too late   to be brand...

Interlude 3

|C#5   Bsus4   E |Asus2 |
   New. _____ Ho,

|C#5   Bsus4   E |Asus2 |
                               oh.

Chorus 3

E
  It's alright, just wait and see.

  Bsus4
Your   string of lights are still bright to me.

  C#m7
Oh,   who you are is not where you've been.

Asus2
  You're still an innocent.

E
  It's okay, ah, life is a tough crowd.

Bsus4
  Thirty-two and still growing up now.

C#m7
  Who you are is not what you did.

Asus2
  You're still an innocent.

Interlude 4

Repeat Interlude 1

Outro

C#5   B/D#   E5   Asus2
  Lost your balance on the tightrope, ___ oh.

C#5   B/D#   E5   A5
  It's never too late to get it back.

Last Kiss

Words and Music by
Taylor Swift

I   still   re-mem - ber   the look on   your _ face, _

(Capo 3rd fret)

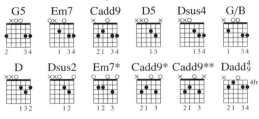

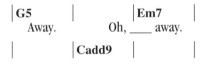

Intro | G5 | | Em7 | |
| | Cadd9 | | |

Verse 1

G5
I still remember the look on your face,

Em7
Lit through the darkness at one-fifty-eight.

Cadd9
The words that you whispered for just us to know.

D5
You told me you loved me, so why did you go...

Interlude | G5 | | Em7 | |
Away.   Oh, ___ away.
| | Cadd9 | | |

Verse 2

G5
I do recall now, the smell of the rain

Em7
Fresh on the pavement. I ran off the plane.

Cadd9
That July ninth, the beat of your heart

Dsus4
It jumps through your shirt. I can still feel your arms.

Pre-Chorus 1

Cadd9   G/B

But now I'll go sit on the floor wearin' your clothes.

                    Cadd9   Dsus4

All that I know is I don't know how to be something you miss.

Chorus 1

D   G5

I never thought we'd have a last kiss.

                         Em7

I never imagined we'd end like this.

Cadd9   Dsus2

Your name, forever the name on my ___ lips.

Verse 3

G5

I do remember the swing of your step.

          Em7

The life of the party, you're showin' off again.

            Cadd9

And I roll my eyes and then you pull me in.

          Dsus2   D

I'm not much for dancin', but for you I did because

Verse 4

G5

I love your handshake meetin' my father.

        Em7

I love how you walk with your hands in your pockets,

              Cadd9

How you'd kiss me when I was in the middle of sayin' somethin'.

          Dsus2   D

There's not a day I don't miss those rude interrup - tions.

Pre-Chorus 2

Cadd9   G/B

And I'll go sit on the floor wearin' your clothes.

                    Cadd9   Dsus4

All that I know is I don't know how to be something you miss.

Chorus 2

    D   **G5**
I never thought we'd have a last kiss.

                 Em7
I never imagined we'd end like this.

Cadd9   **Dsus2**   **D**   **Cadd9** **D**
Your name, forever the name on my ___ lips.   Mm.

Bridge

G5   **Em7***   **Cadd9***
  So I'll watch your life in pictures

    D5   **G5**
Like I used to watch you sleep.

    Em7*   **Cadd9***
And I feel you for - get me

    D5   **G5**
Like I used to feel you breathe.

    Em7*   **Cadd9***
And I'll keep up with our old friends

    D5   **Cadd9****
Just to ask them how you are.

              Dadd$_9^4$
Hope it's nice where you are.

    Cadd9
And I hope the sun shines and it's a beautiful day,

    G/B
And something reminds you, you wish you had stayed.

    Cadd9
You can plan for a change in the weather and time,

    Dsus2
But I never planned on you changin' your mind.

Pre-Chorus 3

Cadd9   **G/B**
So I'll go sit on the floor wearin' your clothes.

                     Cadd9   **Dsus4**
All that I know is I don't know how to be something you miss.

Chorus 3

Repeat Chorus 1

Outro

D   **G5**
  Just like our last kiss.

                       Em7
Forever the name on my ____ lips.

                       Cadd9
Forever the name on my ____ lips.

          G5
Just like our last.

Long Live

Words and Music by
Taylor Swift

Melody:

I said, "Re - mem-ber this mo - ment,"

G5   Cadd9   Em7   Dadd4   C   D/F#

Em   D5/A   Cadd9*   G5*   Em*   D5

Intro

| G5 | | | Cadd9 | | |
| Em7 | Dadd4 | C | | |

Verse 1

   C N.C.   G5
I said, "Remember this mo - ment,"

                         Cadd9
In the back of my mind.

                               Em7
The time we stood with our shak - ing hands,

              D/F#   Cadd9
The crowds ____ in stands went wild.

                           G5
We were the kings and the queens

                       Cadd9
And they read off our names.

                          Em
The night you danced like you knew

               D5/A   C
Our lives would nev - er be the same.

                           Em   Cadd9
You held your head like a he - ro on a hist'ry book page.

                    Em D5/A   Cadd9
It was the end of a dec - ade,   but the start of an age.

Chorus 1

Cadd9* N.C.   G5*   Cadd9*
                   Long live the walls we crashed through.

                 Em*
All the kingdom lights shined just for me and you.

D5   G5*
  I was screamin' long live all the magic we made

Cadd9*   Em*
  And bring on all the pretend - ers.

       Cadd9*   G5*
One day ___ we will be remem - bered.

Verse 2

   N.C.   G5
I said, "Remember this feel - in'!"

                        Cadd9
I passed the pictures around

                    Em
Of all the years that we stood ___there

         D/F♯   Cadd9
On the side - lines wishin' for right ___ now.

                    G5
We are the kings and queens.

                          Cadd9
You traded your baseball cap for a crown.

                   Em
When they gave us our tro - phies

             D5   C
And we held ___ them up for our ___ town.

                    Em   Cadd9
And the cynics were out - raged, screaming, "This is absurd!"

                    Em
'Cause for a moment, a band ___ of thieves

         D5   Cadd9   Cadd9*
In ripped ___ up jeans got to rule ___ the world.

Chorus 2

N.C.   **G5***   **Cadd9***
Long live the walls we crashed through.

                      Em*
All the kingdom lights shined just for me and you.

D5   **G5***
I was screamin' long live all the magic we made,

Cadd9*   **Em***   **D5**
And bring on all the pretend - ers. I'm not afraid.

  G5*
Long live, all the mountains we moved.

Cadd9*   **Em ***   **D5**
I had the time of my life fighting dragons with you.

             G5*   **Cadd9***
I was screamin' long live the look on your face,

                Em*
And bring on all the pretend - ers.

     Cadd9*   **G5***
One day, ___ we will be remem - bered.

Bridge

Cadd9*   **Em***
Hold on, just spinnin' around.

     Cadd9* Em*
Con - fetti   falls to the ground.

     Cadd9*
May these mem'ries break our fall.

G5   **Cadd9**
Will you take a mo - ment, promise me this,

                                    Em7
That you'll stand by me forev - er?

            Dadd4   **C**
But if, God ___ forbid, fate should step in

                        G5   **Cadd9**
And force us into a good - bye, if you have children someday,

                        Em
When they point to the pic - tures,

D5   **Cadd9**
    Please tell 'em my name.

                Cadd9*
Tell 'em how the crowds went wild.

                                D5
Tell 'em how I hope they shine.

Chorus 3

            G5*   **Cadd9***
Long live the walls we crashed through.

                    Em*   **D5**
I had the time of my life with you.

            G5*   **Cadd9***
Long, long live the walls we crashed through.

                        Em*
All the kingdom lights shined just for me and you.

D5   **G5***
    An' I was screamin' long live all the magic we made,

Cadd9*   **Em***   **D5**
    And bring on all the pretend - ers. I'm not afraid.

                G5*   **Cadd9***
Singin' long live all the mountains we moved.

                        Em*   **D5**
I had the time of my life fighting dragons with you.

                G5*   **Cadd9***
And long, long live the look on your face,

                            Em*
And bring on all the pretend - ers.

            Cadd9* N.C.
One day, ___ we will be remembered.

Love Story

Words and Music by
Taylor Swift

Melody:

We were both young when I first saw ___ you.

(Capo 2nd fret)

Intro

| C | | | G5 | | |
| A5 | | | F | | Fsus2 |

Verse 1

C
We were both young when I first saw you.

F
I close my eyes and the flashback starts.

A5   F   Fsus2
I'm standing there on a balcony in summer air.

C
See the lights, see the party, the ball gowns.

F   A5
See you make your way through the crowd and say hel - lo.

G5
Little did I ____ know that

Pre-Chorus 1

F   G5
You were Romeo. You were throwing pebbles

A5   C
And my daddy said, "Stay away from Juliet."

F   G5
And I was crying on the staircase, begging you,

A5 F   G5
"Please don't go." ____   And I ____ said,

Chorus 1

C*
"Romeo, take me somewhere where we can be alone.

G5*
I'll be waiting; all there's left to do is run.

Am
You'll be the prince and I'll be the princess.

F*   **G5***   **N.C.** **C**
It's a love story. Baby, just say   yes."

Verse 2

     C
So I sneak out to the garden to see you.

F
We keep quiet 'cause we're dead if they knew.

          A5   **G5**
So close your eyes, escape this town for a little while.

Oh, oh, 'cause

Pre-Chorus 2

F   **G5**
You were Romeo, I was a scarlet letter

      A5   **C**
And my daddy said, "Stay away from Juliet."

         F
But you were ev'rything to me,

     G5   **A5**
I was beggin' you, "Please don't go."

F   **G5**
  And I ___ said,

Chorus 2

C*
"Romeo, take me somewhere where we can be alone.

G5*
I'll be waiting; all there's left to do is run.

Am
You'll be the prince and I'll be the princess.

F*   **G5***
It's a love story. Baby, just say yes.

C*
Romeo save me. They're try'n' to tell me how to feel.

G5*
  This love is difficult, but it's, uh, real.

Am
Don't be afraid, we'll make it out of this mess.

F*   **G5***
It's a love story. Baby, just say yes."

Guitar Solo | **C*** | | **G5*** | |
                    Oh, oh.

          | **Am** | | **F*** | **G5*** |

Bridge
                  Am
I got tired of waiting,

Fadd9   **C5**   **G5***
  Wondering if you were ever coming around.

                  Am   **Fadd9**
My faith in you was   fading

         C5   **G**
When I met you on the outskirts of town and I said,

Chorus 3

    C
"Romeo save me. I've been feeling so alone.

G5**
I keep waiting for you, but you never come."

    A5
Is this in my head? I don't know what to think.

    F5   **G5*****   **N.C.**
He knelt to the ground and pulled out a ring and said,

Chorus 4

    D
"Marry me, Juliet. You'll never have to be alone.

A
I love you and that's all I really know.

  Bm
I talked to your dad, go pick out a white dress.

G5*   **A**   **D**
It's a love story. Baby, just say   yes."

             A   **Bm**
Oh, oh, oh. ____ Oh, oh, oh, ____ oh.

      G5*   **D**
'Cause we were both young when I first saw you.

Mary's Song
(Oh My My My)

Words and Music by Taylor Swift,
Liz Rose and Brian Maher

Melody:

She _ said,   "I was sev-en and you _ were nine. _

(Capo 2nd fret)

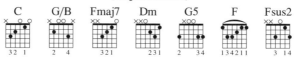

C   G/B   Fmaj7   Dm   G5   F   Fsus2

Intro |C |G/B |Fmaj7 | |

Verse 1

         C
She said,   "I was seven and you were nine.

G/B
I looked at you like the stars that shined

Fmaj7
In the sky, the pretty lights."

       C
And our daddies used to joke about the two of us

G/B
Growing up and falling in love.

    Fmaj7
And our mamas smiled and rolled their eyes

    Dm   **G5**
And said, "Oh, my, my, ___ my."

Chorus 1

N.C.   C
Take me back ____ to the house in the backyard tree.

   G/B
Said you'd beat me up, you were bigger than me.

  F
You never did, you never did.

     C
Take me back ____ when our world was one block wide.

  G/B
I dared ____ you to kiss me and ran when you tried.

F   C   F C F
Just two kids, you and I, oh, my, my, my, my.

Verse 2

  C
Well, I was sixteen when suddenly

 G/B
I wasn't that little girl you used to see,

   F
But your eyes still shined like pretty lights.

   C
And our daddies used to joke about the two of us,

  G/B
They never believed we'd really fall in love.

   F
And our mamas smiled and rolled their eyes

   Dm   G5
And said, "Oh, my, my, ____ my."

Chorus 2

N.C.   C
Take me back ___ to the creek beds we turned up,

G/B
Two a.m. riding in your truck

    F
And all I need is you next to me.

             C
Take me back ___ to the time we had our very first fight,

       G/B
The slam - ming of doors 'stead of kissing goodnight.

      F   Dm
You stayed outside till the morning light.

       C   F   C   F
Oh, my, my, my, my.

Verse 3

C
A few years had gone and come around.

      G/B
We were sitting at our fav'rite spot in town

       Fsus2
And you looked at me, got down on one knee.

Chorus 3

N.C.   C
Take me back ___ to the time when we walked down the aisle.

      G/B
Our whole ___ town came and our mamas cried.

    F
You said, "I do," and I did, too.

           C
Take me home ___ where we met so many years before.

      G/B
We'll rock ___ our babies on that very front porch.

      F
After all this time, you and I.

Outro

    C
And I'll be eighty seven, you'll be eighty nine.

      G/B   F
I'll still look at you like the stars that shine in the sky.

     Dm   C
Oh, my, my, my.

The Outside

Words and Music by
Taylor Swift

Melody:

I did - n't know __

(Capo 5th fret)

C   G5   Dm   F   C5   G5*   Fmaj7   Fsus2   Am

Intro   ‖: C | G5 | Dm | F   :‖

Verse 1

   C5   G5*   Fmaj7
I didn't know ____ what I would find

When I went looking for a reason, I know.

   C5   G5*   Fmaj7
I didn't read ____ between the lines

                                Dm
And, baby, I've got nowhere to go.

                            Fsus2
I tried to take the road less trave - led by,

   Dm   Fsus2
   But nothing seems to work the first few times.

      G5*
Am I right?

	C **G5**

Chorus 1

         C   **G5**
So how ____ can I ever try ____ to be better?

F
Nobody ever lets me in.

  C
I ____ can still see you.

    G5
This ____ ain't the best view,

F
On the outside looking in.

    Dm
I've ____ been a lot of lonely places.

     F   **G5**
I've ____ never been ____ on the outside.

Verse 2

C   **G5**   **F**
  You saw me there, ____ but never knew

                      C   **G5**
That I would give it all up to be ____ a part of this,

      F
A part of you. ____ And now it's all too late.

      Dm   **Fsus2**
So you see, ____ you could've helped if you had want - ed to.

Dm   **Fsus2**   **G5**
  But no one notices until it's too late ____ to do anything.

Chorus 2

        C   **G5**
How ___ can I ever try ___ to be better?

F
Nobody ever lets me in.

  C
I ___ can still see you.

     G5
This ___ ain't the best view,

F
On the outside looking in.

     Dm
I've ___ been a lot of lonely places.

    F   **G5**
I've ___ never been ___ on the outside.

Guitar Solo

| **Am** | | **C** | | **F** | | **C** | | |
Oh, yeah.

| **Am** | | **C** | | **Dm** | | **F** | | | |

Chorus 3

     C5   **G5***
How ___ can I ever try ___ to be better?

Fmaj7
  Nobody ever lets me in.

C5
I ___ can still see you.

  G5*
This ___ ain't the best view,

Fmaj7
  On the outside looking in.

     Dm
I've ___ been a lot of lonely places.

    F   **G5**
I've ___ never been ___ on the outside.

Outro

     C   **G5**   **Dm**
Oh, ___ oh, ___ oh.

F   **C** **G5** **Dm**
  Oh, ___   oh.

Mean

Words and Music by
Taylor Swift

Melody:

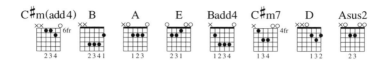

You,   with your words like knives and

| C#m(add4) | B | A | E | Badd4 | C#m7 | D | Asus2 |

Verse 1

C#m(add4)   B   A
You, with your words like knives and swords

And weapons that you use against me,

C#m(add4)   B   A
You have   knocked me off my feet ____ again,

Got me feeling like a nothing.

C#m(add4)   B   A
You, with your voice like nails on a chalkboard,

Calling me out when I'm wounded.

C#m(add4)   B   A
You,   picking on the weaker man.

Pre-Chorus 1

B
  Well, you can take me down

E   A   B
  With just one single blow.

              A
But you ____ don't know what you don't know.

Chorus 1

     E   **Badd4** **C#m7**   **A**
Someday, I'll be   living in a big ol' city,

       E   **Badd4**   **A**
And all you're ever gonna be is mean.

E   **Badd4** **C#m7**   **A**
Someday, I'll be   big enough so you can't hit me,

       E   **Badd4**   **A**
And all you're ever gonna be is mean.

     N.C.   **E**   **D**   **E**
Why you gotta be so ___ mean?

Verse 2

C#m7   **Badd4**
You, with your switching sides

       A
And your wildfire lies and your humiliation,

C#m7 **Badd4**   **A**
You have pointed out my flaws ___ again

         N.C.
As if I don't al - ready see them.

C#m7   **Badd4**
  I walk with my ___ head down

      A
Tryin' to block you out 'cause I'll never impress you.

C#m7 **Badd4**   **A**
I just   wanna feel okay ___ again.

TAYLOR SWIFT   **73**

Pre-Chorus 2

Badd4
I bet you got pushed around,

E   **A**
Somebody made you cold.

Badd4
But the cycle ends right now,

        A
'Cause you __ can't lead me down that road

                       N.C.
And you don't know what you don't ____ know.

Chorus 2

E   **Badd4** **C♯m7**   **A**
Someday, I'll be   living in a big ol' city,

   E   **Badd4**   **A**
And all you're ever gonna be is mean.

E   **Badd4** **C♯m7**   **A**
Someday, I'll be   big enough so you can't hit me,

   E   **Badd4**   **A**
And all you're ever gonna be is mean.

              E   **D** **E** **Badd4**
Why you gotta be so ____ mean?

Mandolin Solo | **Asus2** | **Badd4** | **Asus2** | |

Bridge

     Badd4
And I can see you years from now in a bar,

E   **A**
Talking over a football game,

Badd4   **E**   **A**
With that same big loud opinion but   nobody's listening.

Badd4   **C♯m7**   **Badd4** **Asus2**
Washed up and ranting about the same old bitter   things.

Badd4   **C♯m7** **Badd4** **Asus2**
Drunk and grumblin' on about how I   can't   sing.

Interlude
                                        E   **Badd4**   **C#m7**

But all you are is ____ mean.

A   **E**   **Badd4**

All you are is mean and a liar

     C#m7   **A**

And pa - thetic and a - lone in life

E   **Badd4**   **C#m7**   **A**

And mean, and mean, and mean, and mean.

Chorus 3
                             N.C.

But someday, I'll be living in a big ol' city,

And all you're ever gonna be is mean. Yeah!

E   **Badd4** **C#m7**   **A**

Someday, I'll be   big enough so you can't hit me,

     E   **Badd4**   **A**

And all you're ever gonna be is mean. (Why you gotta be so mean?)

Chorus 4
E   **Badd4** **C#m7**   **A**

Someday, I'll be   living in a big ol' city,

     E   **Badd4**   **A**

And all you're ever gonna be is mean.

E   **Badd4** **C#m7**   **A**

Someday, I'll be   big enough so you can't hit me,

     E   **Badd4**   **A**

And all you're ever gonna be is mean.

                         E

Why you gotta be so ____ mean?

Mine

Words and Music by
Taylor Swift

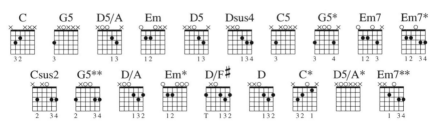

Intro

| N.C. | C G5 D5/A | Em | C G5 D5 |

Ah, ah, ah.

| | C G5 D5/A | Em | C G5 | Dsus4 |

Ah, ah, ah.

Verse 1

C5   G5*   D5   Em7
You were in college, working part time, waiting tables.

C   G5   D5
Left a small town, never looked back.

C   G5*   D5   Em7*
I was a flight risk   with a fear of falling,

C   G5   D5/A
Wond'ring why we bother with love if it never lasts.

Pre-Chorus 1

Csus2 G5** D/A
    I say, "Can you believe it?"

Csus2 G5** D/A   Csus2
    As we're lying on the couch.

G5** D/A   Csus2 G5**
The moment, I can see it. Yes, yes.

D/A
I can see it now.

Chorus 1

Csus2   **G5****
  Do you remember? We were sitting there by the water.

D/A   **Em***   **D/F♯**
  You put your arm around me ___ for the first time.

Csus2   **G5****
  You made a rebel of a careless man's careful daughter.

D/A   **Em7***   **D/F♯**   **Csus2**
  You are the best thing   that's ever been mine.

Verse 2

Csus2 G5**   **D**   **Em***
  Flash ___ forward and we're taking on the world together

Csus2   **G5****   **D**
  And there's a drawer of my things at your place.

Csus2   **G5****   **D**   **Em***
  You learn my secrets and you figure out why I'm guarded.

Csus2   **G5****   **D**
  You say we'll never make my parents' mistakes.

Pre-Chorus 2

Csus2 G5** D   **Csus2 G5** D**
       But we got bills to pay.

        Csus2 G5** D
We got nothing figured out.

        Csus2 G5**
When it was hard to take, yes,   yes,

D
This is what I thought about.

Chorus 2

Csus2   G5**
Do you remember? We were sitting there by the water.

D/A   Em*   D/F#
You put your arm around me ___ for the first time.

Csus2   G5**
You made a rebel of a careless man's careful daughter.

D/A   Em7*   D/F#
You are the best thing   that's ever been mine.

Csus2   G5**
Do you remember all the city lights on the water?

D/A   Em*   D/F#
You saw me start to believe ___ for the first time.

Csus2   G5**
You made a rebel of a careless man's careful daughter.

D/A   Em7*   D/F#
You are the best thing   that's ever been mine.

Interlude |Csus2 G5** D/A | Em* |Csus2* G5** D/A | |
                              Uh, oh, oh.

Bridge

               Em*   C*
And I re - member that fight, two thirty A.M.

               D   Dsus4 D
You said ev'rything was slip - ping

          Dsus4   D
Right ___ out of our ___ hands.

        Em*
I ___ ran out crying and you

C*   D   Dsus4 D   Dsus4 D
Followed me out into the street.

Pre-Chorus 3

Csus2 G5**   D   Csus2
          Braced my - self for the goodbye

G5**   D   Csus2
'Cause that's all I've ever known.

G5** D   Csus2
And you took me by surprise.

G5**   D   Csus2
You said, "I'll never leave you a - lone."

Chorus 3

                    C   G5
You said,   "I remember how we felt, sitting by the water.

D5/A*   Em7**   D5
And ev'ry time I look at you,   it's like the first time.

Csus2   G5**
I fell in love with a careless man's careful daughter.

D
She is the best thing that's ever been mine."

Chorus 4

    Csus2   G5**   D/A   Em*   D/F♯
(Hold on and make it last. Hold on, never turn back.)

Csus2   G5**
You made a rebel of a careless man's careful daughter.

D/A
You are the best thing that's ever been mine.

Outro

Csus2 G5** D/A   Em*
          Do you be - lieve it?

Csus2 G5** D/A
          We're gonna make it, now.

Csus2 G5** D/A   Em*
          And I can see it.

Csus2 G5** D/A
          I can see it now.

Never Grow Up

Words and Music by Taylor Swift

(Capo 7th fret)

Intro

| G5 D/F# | Em D5 | C | D5 | |
| G5 D/F# | Em D5 | Cadd9 | | |

Verse 1

> G5   D/F#   Em   D5
> Your little hand's wrapped a - round my finger
>
>   Cadd9   D5
> And it's   so quiet in the world tonight.
>
> G5   D/F# Em   D5
> Your little eyelids flutter 'cause you're dreamin',
>
>   Cadd9   D5
> So I   tuck you in, turn on your fav'rite nightlight.

Pre-Chorus 1

> Cadd9   Em7   Cadd9
> To you ev'rything's funny.   You got nothing to regret.
>
>   D5   Dsus2   D
> I'd give all I have, honey,   if you could stay ____ like that.

GUITAR CHORD SONGBOOK

Chorus 1

G5 D/F♯   Em D5
Oo, darlin', don't you ever grow up.

   Cadd9   D5 G5/D
Don't you ever grow up. Just stay this lit - tle.

G5 D/F♯   Em D5
 Oo, darlin', don't you ever grow up.

     C   D
Don't you ever grow up. It could stay this simple.

Cadd9
 I won't let nobody hurt you,

Em7   Cadd9
 Won't let no one break your heart.

And no one will desert you.

D   G5 D/F♯ Em D5 C
 Just try to never grow up.

Dsus2 G5/D G5 D/F♯ Em D5 Cadd9 D5
 And nev - er grow up.

G5   D/F♯ Em   D5
 You're in the car on the way to the movies

Verse 2

      C   D5
And you're mortified your mom's droppin' you off.

G5   D/F♯   Em   D5
 At fourteen, ___ there's just so much you can't do,

    Cadd9   D5
And you can't wait to move out someday and call your own shots.

Cadd9
 But don't make her drop you off around the block.

Pre-Chorus 2

Em7*   Cadd9
 Remember that she's getting older too.

           Dsus2
And don't lose the way that you dance around

          D5/A G5/D
In your PJ's getting ready for school.

Chorus 2

G5   D/F♯   Em   D5
  Oo, darlin', don't you ever grow up.

           Cadd9   D5   G5/D
Don't you ever grow up. Just stay this little.

G5   D/F♯   Em   D5
  Oo, darlin', don't you ever grow up.

            C   D5
Don't you ever grow up. It could stay this simple.

Cadd9
And no one's ever burned you.

Em7   Cadd9
Nothin's ever left you scarred.

                  D5
And even though you want to,

Dsus2 D   G5 D/F♯ Em D5 Cadd9 D5
  Just try to never grow up.

Bridge

Cadd9*   G/B   D/A Dsus4/A
  Take pictures in your mind ___ of your childhood room.

Cadd9*   G/B   D/A
  Memorize what it sound - ed like when your dad ___ gets home.

      Dsus4/A   Cadd9*   G/B
Re - member the foot - steps, remember the words ___ said

         D/A   Dsus4/A
And all your little brother's fav'rite songs.

Cadd9*   G/B   D5   Dsus2 D
  I just realized ev - 'rything I have ___ is someday gonna be gone.

Verse 3

G5   D/F♯   Em   D5
  So, here I am in my   new a - partment

      C   D5
In a   big city, they just dropped me off.

G5   D/F♯   Em   D5
  It's so much colder than I   thought it would be,

      C   D5
So I tuck myself in and turn my nightlight on.

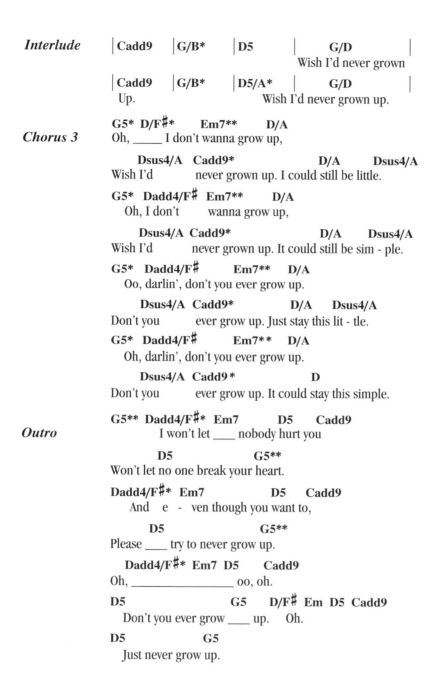

Interlude | Cadd9 | G/B* | D5 | G/D |
                                  Wish I'd never grown

               | Cadd9 | G/B* | D5/A* | G/D |
                Up.   Wish I'd never grown up.

               G5* D/F#*   Em7**   D/A
Chorus 3   Oh, _____ I don't wanna grow up,

                     Dsus4/A Cadd9*   D/A   Dsus4/A
               Wish I'd   never grown up. I could still be little.

               G5* Dadd4/F# Em7**   D/A
               Oh, I don't   wanna grow up,

                     Dsus4/A Cadd9*   D/A   Dsus4/A
               Wish I'd   never grown up. It could still be sim - ple.

               G5* Dadd4/F#   Em7**   D/A
               Oo, darlin', don't you ever grow up.

                     Dsus4/A Cadd9*   D/A   Dsus4/A
               Don't you   ever grow up. Just stay this lit - tle.

               G5* Dadd4/F#   Em7**   D/A
               Oh, darlin', don't you ever grow up.

                     Dsus4/A Cadd9 *   D
               Don't you   ever grow up. It could stay this simple.

               G5** Dadd4/F#* Em7   D5   Cadd9
Outro   I won't let ____ nobody hurt you

                   D5   G5**
             Won't let no one break your heart.

             Dadd4/F#* Em7   D5   Cadd9
              And   e - ven though you want to,

                 D5   G5**
             Please ____ try to never grow up.

              Dadd4/F#* Em7 D5   Cadd9
             Oh, _____ oo, oh.

             D5   G5   D/F#   Em D5 Cadd9
             Don't you ever grow ____ up.   Oh.

             D5   G5
             Just never grow up.

Our Song

Words and Music by
Taylor Swift

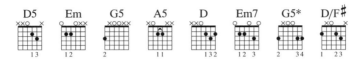

I was rid-ing shot-gun with my hair un-done

D5   Em   G5   A5   D   Em7   G5*   D/F#

Intro   ‖: D5   Em | G5   A5   :‖

Verse 1

       D5   Em
I was riding shotgun with my hair undone

     G5   A5
In the front seat of his car.

        D5   Em
He's got a one hand feel on the ___ steering wheel,

     G5   A5
The other on my   heart.

D5   Em
  I look around, turn the radio down.

        G5   A5
He says, "Baby, is something wrong?"

     D5   Em   G5   A5
I say "Nothing. I was just thinking how we don't have a song."

Chorus 1

N.C.   D   Em7
And he says,   "Our song is the slammin' screen door,

G5*   A5
Sneakin' out late, tapping on your window,

D   Em7   G5*
  When we're on the phone ___ and you talk real ___ slow

                A5   D
'Cause it's late and your mama don't know.

         Em7   G5
Our song is the way you laugh, the first date.

        A5
'Man, I didn't kiss her and I should have.'

G5*   A5   Em7
  And when I got home, 'fore I said a - men,

          D/F# G5* N.C.   D   Em7   G5*   A5
Asking God ___ if He   could play it again."

Verse 2

D5   Em
  I was walking out the front porch steps

    G5   A5
After ___ ev'rything that ___ day

   D5   Em
Had gone all wrong and been trampled on

    G5   A5
And, uh, lost and thrown a - way.

D5   Em
Got to the hallway, well on my way

G5   A5
To my lovin' bed.

  D5   Em
I almost didn't notice all the roses

G5   A5
And the note that   said…

Chorus 2

D   Em7
"Our song is the slammin' screen door,

G5*   A5
Sneakin' out late, tapping on your window,

D   Em7   G5*
When we're on the phone ___ and you talk real ___ slow

        A5   D
'Cause it's late and your mama don't know.

      Em7   G5
Our song is the way you laugh, the first date.

    A5
'Man, I didn't kiss her and I should have.'

G5*   A5   Em7
And when I got home, 'fore I said a - men,

     D/F♯ G5*   A5
Asking God ___ if He could play it again."

Fiddle &
Guitar Solos |D Em7 |G5* A5 |D Em7 |²₄G5* |
           Da, da, da, da.

     |⁴₄A5 |

     Em*   G5*
Bridge I've heard ev'ry album, listened to the radio,

     D   A5   Em*
Wait - ed for some - thing to come along

        G5*
That was as good as our song.

Chorus 3

D5   Em
'Cause our song is the slammin' screen door,

G5   A5   D5
Sneakin' out late, tapping on his, uh, win - dow

                      Em   G5
When we're on the phone ___ and he talks real ___ slow

     A5   D
'Cause it's late and his mama don't know.

         Em7   G5*
Our song is the way he laughs, the first date.

         A5
"Man, I didn't kiss him and I should have."

G5*   A5   Em7
And when I got home, 'fore I said a - men,

        D/F♯ G5*   A5   D Em7   G5*
Asking God ___ if He could play it again, ___ yeah.

A5   D Em7 G5* A5   D
Uh, play it a - gain, _____ oh, yeah.

Em7   G5*   A5
Huh, oh, ___ yeah.

Outro

     D5   Em
I was riding shotgun with my hair undone

     G5   A5
In the front seat of his car.

D5   Em
I grabbed a pen and an old napkin

     G5*
And I   wrote down our song.

Picture to Burn

Words and Music by
Taylor Swift and Liz Rose

Melody:

State the ob - vi - ous, _

G5 Am7 C D5 Cadd9 G/B

Intro | G5 Am7 | C D5 G5 | Am7 | C D5 G5 |

Verse 1
G5   Am7 C   D5   G5
State the ob - vious, I didn't get my per - fect fanta - sy.

   Am7   C   D5
I realize ____ you love yourself ____ more than you could ev - er love me.

G5   Am7   C   D5   G5
So go and tell your friends ____ that I'm ob - sessive and crazy.

   Am7   C   D5   Cadd9
That's fine, you won't mind if I say, and by the way,

Chorus 1
     G5   Am7   C   D5
I hate that stupid old pickup truck you never let me drive.

     G5   Am7   C   D5
You're a redneck heartbreak who's really bad at lyin'.

G5   Am7   C   D5
So watch me strike a match ____ on all my wasted time.

  C   D5   G5 Am7 C D5
As far as I'm concerned, you're just another picture to burn.

Verse 2
G5   Am7   C   D5   G5
 There's no time ____ for tears, I'm just sittin' here plannin' my re - venge.

     Am7   C
There's nothin' stop - pin' me from goin' out

   D5   G5
With all ____ of your best ____ friends.

    Am7   C   D5 G5
And if you come around ____ sayin' sor - ry to me,

    Am7   C   D5
My daddy's gonna show you how sorry you'll be.

Chorus 2

           G5   Am7   C   D5
'Cause I hate that stupid old pickup truck you never let me drive.

        G5   Am7   C   D5
You're a redneck heartbreak who's really bad at lyin'.

G5   Am7   C   D5
   So watch me strike a match ____ on all my wasted time.

    C   D5
As far as I'm concerned, you're just another picture to burn.

Guitar Solo

| G5 Am7 | C   D5 | G5 Am7 | $\frac{2}{4}$C | $\frac{4}{4}$D5 | |

Bridge

    C   D5
And if you're missin' me, you better keep it to yourself

     C   G/B   D5
'Cause comin' back around here would be bad for your health.

Chorus 3

          G   Am7   C   D5
'Cause I hate that stupid old pickup truck you never let me drive.

       G   Am7   C   D5
You're a redneck heartbreak who's really bad at lyin'.

G   Am7   C   D5
   So watch me strike a match ____ on all my wasted time.

    C   D5
In case you haven't heard, I really, really hate that

Chorus 4

G5   Am7   C   D5
Stupid old pickup truck you never let me drive.

        G5   Am7   C   D5
You're a redneck heartbreak who's really bad at lyin'.

G5   Am7   C   D5
   So watch me strike a match ____ on all my wasted time.

    C   D5
As far as I'm concerned, you're just another picture to burn.

Outro

G5 Am7 C   D5   G5
            Burn, burn, burn baby, burn.

Am7   C   D5   G5 Am7
  You're just another picture to burn.

C D5   G5
   Baby, burn.

A Place in this World

Words and Music by Taylor Swift,
Robert Ellis Orrall and Angelo

(Capo 2nd fret)

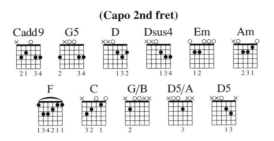

Verse 1

      Cadd9   **G5**   **D**
    I don't know what I want, ____ so don't ask ____ me

          Cadd9   **D**
'Cause I'm still ____ try'n' to figure it out.

           Dsus4   **G5**
Don't know what's down this road.

         D   **Dsus4**   **Cadd9**
I'm just walk - ing, try'n' to see

                 D
Through the rain coming down

        Em   **Cadd9**
Even though ____ I'm not the on - ly one

    G5   **D**
Who feels ____ the way I do.

Chorus 1

N.C.   **Em**   **Cadd9**
I'm alone ___ on my own,

      G5   **D**
And that's all ___ I know.

       Em   **Cadd9**
I'll be strong, ___ I'll be wrong,

      G5   **D**
Oh, but life ___ goes on.

        Am
Oh, I'm just a girl,

F   **C**   **G5**   **D Em**
Try'n' to find a place in this ___ world.

Verse 2

C   **G5**   **D**
  Got the radio on, ___ my old blue ___ jeans,

      Cadd9   **D**
And I'm wear - ing my heart on my sleeve.

      G5   **D**
Feeling lucky today, ___ got the sun - shine.

     Cadd9   **D**
Could you tell ___ me, what more do I need?

     Em   **Cadd9**
And tomor - row's just a mys - tery,

    G5   **D**
Oh, yeah, ___ but that's okay.

Chorus 2

     Em   **Cadd9**
I'm alone ___ on my own,

      G5   **D**
And that's all ___ I know.

      Em   **Cadd9**
I'll be strong, ___ I'll be wrong,

      G5   **D**
Oh, but life ___ goes on.

      Am
Oh, I'm just a girl,

F   **C**   **G5**   **D Em C**
Try'n' to find a place in this ___ world.

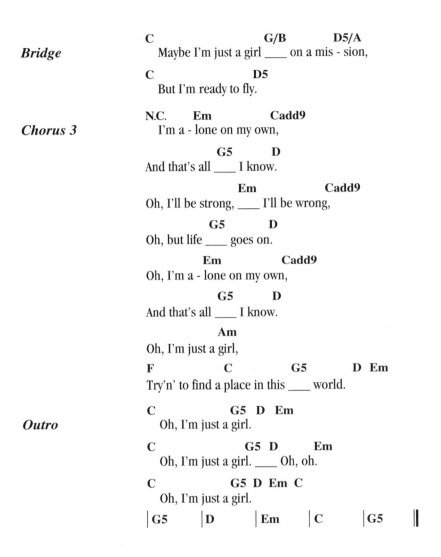

Bridge

  C   G/B   D5/A
  Maybe I'm just a girl ____ on a mis - sion,

  C   D5
  But I'm ready to fly.

Chorus 3

  N.C. **Em**   **Cadd9**
  I'm a - lone on my own,

       G5   **D**
 And that's all ____ I know.

        Em   **Cadd9**
 Oh, I'll be strong, ____ I'll be wrong,

      G5   **D**
 Oh, but life ____ goes on.

       Em   **Cadd9**
 Oh, I'm a - lone on my own,

      G5   **D**
 And that's all ____ I know.

       Am
 Oh, I'm just a girl,

 F   **C**   **G5**   **D Em**
 Try'n' to find a place in this ____ world.

Outro

  C   **G5 D Em**
  Oh, I'm just a girl.

  C   **G5 D**   **Em**
  Oh, I'm just a girl. ____ Oh, oh.

  C   **G5 D Em C**
  Oh, I'm just a girl.

 | G5 |D | Em | C |G5   ‖

Should've Said No

Words and Music by
Taylor Swift

It's strange to think the songs _ we used _ to sing, _

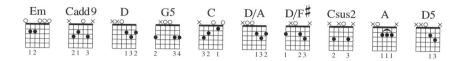

Em Cadd9 D G5 C D/A D/F# Csus2 A D5

Intro

| Em   Cadd9 | D   G5 | Em   Cadd9 | D |
| Em   C | D/A   G5 D/F# | Em   C | D/A |

Verse 1

G5   D/F#   Em
  It's strange to think the songs ___ we used to sing,

                    C   G5   D/F# Em C
The smiles, the flow - ers, ev'rything ___ is gone.

G5   D/F#   Em
  Yesterday I found out about you,

                    C   G5   D/F# Em C
Even now just looking at you ___ feels wrong.

Em   C   G5
  You say that you'd take it all back given one ___ chance,

                D/A   C   D/A
It was a moment of   weakness and you ___ said yes.

Chorus 1

        N.C.   **Em**   **C**

You should've said no, you should've gone home.

                        D/A   **G5**

You should've thought twice 'fore you let it all go.

      D/F♯   **Em**   **C**

You should've known that word 'bout what you did with her

                      D/A

Would get back to me. ____ (Get back to me.)

                    Em   **C**

And I should've been there in the back of your mind,

              D/A   **G5**

I shouldn't be asking myself why.

      D/F♯   **Em**   **Csus2**   **A**

You shouldn't be begging for forgive - ness at my feet.

                   C   **D5**

You should've said no, baby, and you might still have me.

Interlude |**Em**   **C** |**D/A**   **G5 D/F♯** |**Em**   **C** |**D/A** |

Verse 2

G5   **D/F♯**

  You can see that I've ____ been crying

Em   **C**   **G5**   **D/F♯ Em**

  And, baby, you know all ____ the right things ____ to say.

C   **G5**   **D/F♯**   **Em**   **C**   **G5**

  But do you honestly ex - pect me to believe

          D/F♯   **Em** **C**

We could ever be the same?

Em   **C**

  You say that the past is the past.

             G5   **D/A**

You need one ____ chance, it was a moment of   weakness

          C   **D/A**

And you ____ said yes.

Chorus 2   *Repeat Chorus 1*

Guitar Solo | G5 D/F♯ | Em C | G5 D/F♯ | C |

Bridge

Em   C   A
I can't resist, ___ before you go, tell me this,

          C   D5   C
Was it   worth it? ___ Was she ___ worth this?

Em C   D5/A
No, ___ mm, no,

G5   D/F♯   Em C   D/A
No, no, ___ no, _____ mm, no.

N.C.   Em   C
Chorus 3   You should've said no, you should've gone home.

                              D/A   G5
You should've thought twice 'fore you let it all go.

          D/F♯   Em   C
You should've known that word 'bout what you did with her

                              D/A
Would get back to me. ___ (Get back to me.)

                          Em   C
And I should've been there in the back of your mind,

                      D/A   G5
I shouldn't be asking myself why.

          D/F♯   Em   Csus2   A
You shouldn't be begging for forgive - ness at my feet.

                          C   D5   Em
You should've said no, baby, and you might still have me.

Sparks Fly

Words and Music by
Taylor Swift

Melody:

The way you move is like a full - on __ rain __ storm

(Capo 5th fret)

Am7   Fsus2   C   Gadd4   Gadd4/B

Intro   ‖: **Am7** | **Fsus2** | **C** | **Gadd4** :‖

Verse 1

Am7   **Fsus2**
The way you move is like a full-on rain storm

C   **Gadd4**
And I'm a house of cards.

                Am7   **Fsus2**
You're the   kinda reckless that should send me runnin'

          C   **Gadd4**
But I   kinda know that I won't get far.

Pre-Chorus 1

Fsus2   **Gadd4**
And you stood there in front ___ of me

          C   **Gadd4/B**   **Am7**
Just   close e - nough to touch.

Fsus2   **Gadd4**
Close enough to hope you couldn't see ___ what I was thinking of.

Chorus 1

N.C.   **Am7**   **Fsus2**
Drop ev'rything now. Meet me in the pouring rain.

C   **Gadd4**
Kiss me on the sidewalk, take away the pain.

       Am7 Fsus2   **C**   **Gadd4**
'Cause I see   sparks fly when - ever you smile.

           Am7   **Fsus2**
Get me with those green eyes, baby, as the lights go down.

       C   **Gadd4**
Give me somethin' that'll haunt me when ____ you're not around.

      Am7 Fsus2   **C** **Gadd4**   **Am7 Fsus2 C Gadd4**
'Cause I see   sparks fly when - ever you ____ smile.

Verse 2

Am7   **Fsus2**
  My mind forgets ____ to remind me

C   **Gadd4**
  You're a bad ide - a.

Am7   **Fsus2**
  You touch me once and it's   really somethin',

        C   **Gadd4**
You find ____ I'm even better than you   imagined I would be.

Fsus2   **Gadd4**
  I'm on my guard for the rest of the world

        C   **Gadd4/B**   **Am7**
But with you, ____ I know it's no good.

Fsus2   **Gadd4**
  And I could wait patiently but   I really wish you would…

Chorus 2   *Repeat Chorus 1*

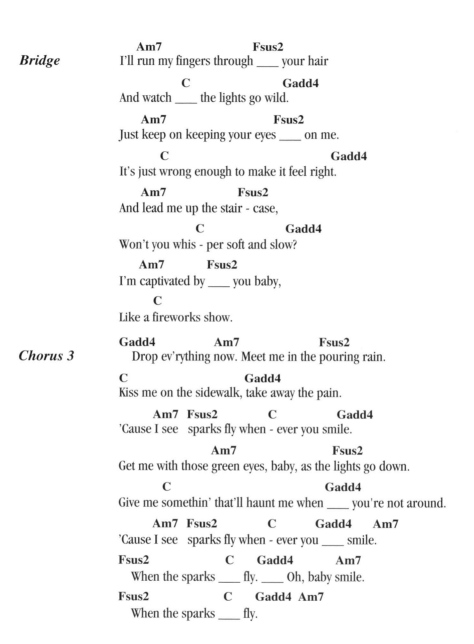

Bridge

      Am7   Fsus2

I'll run my fingers through ____ your hair

            C   Gadd4

And watch ____ the lights go wild.

      Am7   Fsus2

Just keep on keeping your eyes ___ on me.

            C   Gadd4

It's just wrong enough to make it feel right.

      Am7   Fsus2

And lead me up the stair - case,

            C   Gadd4

Won't you whis - per soft and slow?

      Am7   Fsus2

I'm captivated by ___ you baby,

        C

Like a fireworks show.

Chorus 3

Gadd4   Am7   Fsus2

  Drop ev'rything now. Meet me in the pouring rain.

C   Gadd4

Kiss me on the sidewalk, take away the pain.

    Am7 Fsus2   C   Gadd4

'Cause I see sparks fly when - ever you smile.

              Am7   Fsus2

Get me with those green eyes, baby, as the lights go down.

       C   Gadd4

Give me somethin' that'll haunt me when ___ you're not around.

    Am7 Fsus2   C   Gadd4   Am7

'Cause I see sparks fly when - ever you ___ smile.

Fsus2   C   Gadd4   Am7

When the sparks ___ fly. ___ Oh, baby smile.

Fsus2   C   Gadd4 Am7

When the sparks ___ fly.

Stay Beautiful

Words and Music by
Taylor Swift and Liz Rose

Melody:

Cor-y's eyes ___ are like a jun-gle.

(Capo 1st fret)

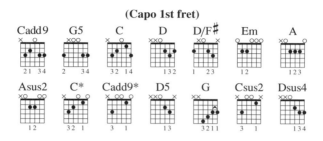

Cadd9   G5   C   D   D/F♯   Em   A

Asus2   C*   Cadd9*   D5   G   Csus2   Dsus4

Intro | Cadd9 | G5 | Cadd9 | G5 |

               C   D

Verse 1   Cory's eyes ___ are like a jungle.

                      G5   D/F♯   Em

He smiles, ___ it's like the ___ radio.

                C   D

He whispers songs ___ into my window

                      G5   D/F♯   Em

In words ___ that no - body knows.

                C   D

There's pretty girls ___ on ev'ry corner,

                      G5   D/F♯   Em

They watch ___ him as he's ___ walking home,

                                   A   Asus2   C* D

Saying, "Does he know?" ___   Will you ever know?

Chorus 1

G5
You're beautiful, ev'ry little piece, love.

Em   C*   Cadd9*
And don't you know you're really gonna be some - one?

C*   D
Ask anyone.

G5
And when you find ev'rything you looked for,

Em   C*   Cadd9*
I hope your life leads you back to my door.

C*   D   Cadd9 G5 Cadd9 G5
Oh, but if it don't, ____ stay beautiful.

Verse 2

C   D   G5   D/F♯   Em
Cory finds ____ another way to be the highlight of ____ my day.

C   D   G5   D/F♯   Em
I'm taking pic - tures in my mind so I can save 'em for a rainy day.

C   D
It's hard to make ____ a conversation

      G5   D/F♯   Em
When he's taking my breath ____ away.

             A   Asus2   C* D
I should say, ____ hey, by the way…

Chorus 2

G5
You're beautiful, ev'ry little piece, love.

Em   C*   Cadd9*
And don't you know you're really gonna be some - one?

C*   D
Ask anyone.

G5
And when you find ev'rything you looked for,

Em   C*   Cadd9*
I hope your life leads you back to my door.

C*   D   Cadd9 G5 Cadd9 D5
Oh, but if it don't, ____ stay beautiful.

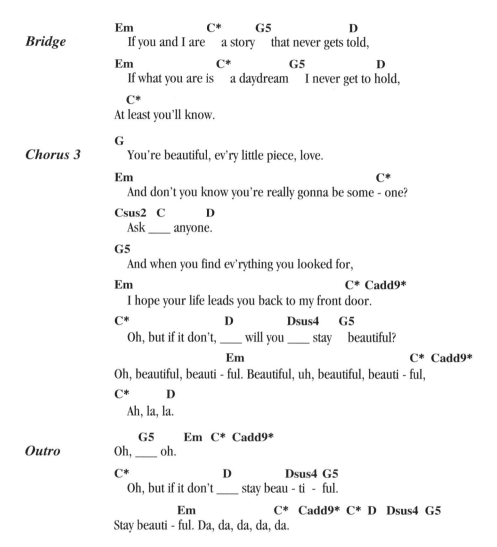

Bridge

Em   C*   G5   D
If you and I are   a story   that never gets told,

Em   C*   G5   D
If what you are is   a daydream   I never get to hold,

C*
At least you'll know.

Chorus 3

G
You're beautiful, ev'ry little piece, love.

Em   C*
And don't you know you're really gonna be some - one?

Csus2 C   D
Ask ___ anyone.

G5
And when you find ev'rything you looked for,

Em   C* Cadd9*
I hope your life leads you back to my front door.

C*   D   Dsus4   G5
Oh, but if it don't, ___ will you ___ stay   beautiful?

                       Em   C* Cadd9*
Oh, beautiful, beauti - ful. Beautiful, uh, beautiful, beauti - ful,

C*   D
Ah, la, la.

Outro

  G5   Em C* Cadd9*
Oh, ___ oh.

C*   D   Dsus4 G5
Oh, but if it don't ___ stay beau - ti - ful.

          Em   C* Cadd9* C* D Dsus4 G5
Stay beauti - ful. Da, da, da, da, da.

Speak Now

Words and Music by
Taylor Swift

Melody:

I am not the kind of girl

G5   D/F#   Am   C   D   Em

Intro

| G5 | | |

Verse 1

G5   D/F#
I am not the kind of girl who should be

Am   C
Rudely bargin' in on a white veil occasion.

G5   D/F#
But you are not the kind of boy

                  Am   C
Who should be marryin' the wrong girl.

Verse 2

G5   D/F#
I sneak in and see your friends

        Am   C
And her snotty little family all dressed in pastel.

        G   D/F#
And she is yelling at a bridesmaid

                    Am
Somewhere back inside a room

                    C
Wearing a gown ____ shaped like a pastry.

GUITAR CHORD SONGBOOK

Pre-Chorus 1

Am C G5   D/F♯
This is surely not what you thought it would be.

Am C   D
I   lose myself in a daydream where I stand and say,

Chorus 1

G5   D/F♯
"Don't say yes, run away now.

  Am   C
I'll meet you when you're out of the church at the back door.

G5   D/F♯
Don't wait or say a single vow.

  Am   C   N.C.
You need to hear me out." And they said, "Speak now."

Interlude 1

|G5 |D/F♯ |Am |C |

Verse 3

G5   D/F♯
Fond gestures are ex - changed

     Am
And the organ starts to play a song

   C
That sounds like a death march.

   G5   D/F♯
And I am hiding in the curtains.

       Am   C
It seems that I was uninvited by your lovely bride-to-be.

Pre-Chorus 2

Am C   G5
She floats down the aisle like a pageant queen.

D/F♯ Am C   D
But I   know you wish it was me.

               N.C.
You wish it was me, ___ *don't you?*

Chorus 2

G5   **D**
Don't say yes, run away now.

  Am   **C**
I'll meet you when you're out of the church at the back door.

G5   **D**
Don't wait or say a single vow.

  Am   **C**
You need to hear me out. And they said, "Speak now."

G5   **D**
Don't say yes, run away now.

  Am   **C**
I'll meet you when you're out of the church at the back door.

G5   **D**
Don't wait or say a single vow.

  Am   **C**
Your time is running out. And they said, "Speak now."

Interlude 2

G5	**D/F♯**	**Am**	**C**	
	A, oo.	La, da, um.		
G5	**D/F♯**	**Am**	**C**	
	A, oo.	Oo.		

Bridge

Em   **C**   **G5**   **D**
I hear the preacher say, "Speak now or forever hold your peace."

Am
There's the silence, there's my last chance.

C   **D**
I stand up with shaky hands, all eyes on me.

Pre-Chorus 3

Am   **C**
Horrified looks from ev'ryone in the room

  D
But I'm only lookin' at you.

Verse 4

G5   D/F♯
I am not the kind of girl who should be

Am   C
Rudely bargin' in on a white veil occasion.

  G5   D/F♯
But you are not the kind of boy

             Am   C
Who should be marryin' the wrong girl, ___ *he, he.*

Chorus 3

G5   D
  So, don't say yes, run away now.

  Am   C
I'll meet you when you're out of the church at the back door.

G5   D
  Don't wait or say a single vow.

   Am   C
You need to hear me out. And they said, "Speak now."

G5   D/F♯
  And you say, "Let's run away now.

  Am   C
I'll meet you when I'm out of my tux at the back door.

G5   D/F♯
  Baby, I didn't say my vows.

  Am   C   G5
So glad you were around when they said, 'Speak now.'"

The Story of Us

Words and Music by
Taylor Swift

Melody:

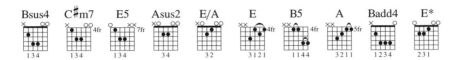

I used to think one ___ day ___ we'd tell the

Bsus4   C#m7   E5   Asus2   E/A   E   B5   A   Badd4   E*

Intro

‖: Bsus4 |C#m7   E5 |
|Asus2   E/A   Asus2   E/A |
|Asus2   E/A   Asus2   E/A Asus2 :‖

Verse 1

E   B5
I used to think one day ____ we'd tell the story of us,

A
How we met and the sparks flew instantly

E   B5   A
And people would say, ____ "They're the lucky ones."

E   B5
I used to know my place ___ was the spot next to you,

A
Now I'm searchin' the room for an empty seat

E   B5   A
'Cause lately I don't even know what page you're on.

Pre-Chorus 1

Badd4   C#m7
Oh, a simple compli - cation,

E5   Asus2   E*
Miscommuni - cations lead to fallout.

Asus2
So many things that I wish you knew.

Badd4   N.C.
So many walls up, I can't break through.

Chorus 1

E*   Badd4
Now I'm standing alone

             Asus2
In a crowded room ____ and we're not speakin'.

E*   Badd4
And I'm dyin' to know,

           Asus2
Is it killing you ____ like it's killin' me? Yeah.

C#m7   Badd4
I don't know what to say

           E*   Asus2
Since the twist of fate when it all broke down.

        C#m7   Badd4   Asus2 E/A Asus2 E/A
And the story of us looks a lot like a tragedy now.

Asus2 N.C.
Next chapter.

Interlude 1

| Bsus4 | C#m7 E5 | Asus2 E/A Asus2 E/A |
| Asus2   E/A   Asus2   E/A Asus2 |

Verse 2

E*   Bsus4
How'd we end up this way?

            Asus2
See me nervously pul - ling at my clothes and tryin' to look busy

E*   Bsus4   Asus2
And you're doin' your best ____ to avoid me.

E*   Bsus4
I'm starting to think one day ____ I'll tell the story of us

Asus2
How I was losing my mind when I saw you here.

E*   Bsus4   Asus2
But you held your pride ____ like you should've held ____ me.

Pre-Chorus 2

Bsus4   C#m7
Oh, I'm scared to see the ending.

E5   Asus2   E*
Why are we pre - tending this is nothin'?

    Asus2
I'd tell you I miss you, but I don't know how.

Bsus4   N.C.
I've never heard silence quite this loud.

Chorus 2

E*   Badd4
  Now I'm standing alone

              Asus2
In a crowded room ____ and we're not speakin'.

E*   Badd4
  And I'm dyin' to know,

        Asus2
Is it killing you ____ like it's killin' me? Yeah.

C#m7   Badd4
  I don't know what to say

        E*   Asus2
Since the twist of fate when it all broke down.

      C#m7
And the story of us

      Badd4   Asus2 E/A Asus2 E/A Asus2 E/A
Looks a lot like a tragedy now.

Guitar Solo

‖: Bsus4 |C#m7 E5 |Asus2 | :‖

Bridge

E*   Asus2
  This is looking like a contest   of who can act like they care less,

  C#m7   Bsus4   Asus2
But I liked it better when you were on my side.

E*   Asus2
  The battle's in your hands now,   but I would lay my armor down

C#m7   Bsus4   Asus2
If you said you'd rather love than fight.

So many things that you wish I knew,

      Bsus4   N.C.
But the story of us might be end - ing soon.

Chorus 3

E* N.C.   **Bsus4**
    Now I'm standing alone

N.C.   **A5**
In a crowded room ____ and we're not speakin'.

E*   **Badd4**
   And I'm dyin' to know,

            Asus2
Is it killing you ____ like it's killin' me? Yeah.

C♯m7   **Badd4**
   I don't know what to say

           E*   **Asus2**
Since the twist of fate when it all broke down.

        C♯m7   **Badd4**   **Asus2**
And the story of us looks a lot like a tragedy now.

E/A Asus2 E/A Asus2   **E/A Asus2 E/A Asus2**
Now, _____ now.

Outro-Chorus

   E* Bsus4 Asus2
            And we're not speakin'

E*   **Bsus4**   **Asus2**
   And I'm dyin' to know, ____ is it killin' you

Like it's killin' me? Yeah.

C♯m7   **Bsus4**
   I don't know what to say

           E*   **Asus2**
Since the twist of fate, 'cause we're goin' down.

        C♯m7   **Bsus4**   **Asus2** **E/A Asus2 E/A**
And the story of us looks a lot like a tragedy now.

Asus2
   The end.

Teardrops on My Guitar

Words and Music by Taylor Swift
and Liz Rose

Drew   looks __   at   me. __

(Capo 3rd fret)

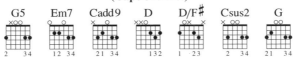

G5   Em7   Cadd9   D   D/F♯   Csus2   G

Intro | G5 | Em7 | Cadd9 | D |

| G5   Em7   Cadd9
Verse 1   Drew looks ____ at me.

      D/F♯   **G5**
I fake ____ a smile so he won't see

           Em7   **Cadd9**
That I want ____ and I'm need - ing

   D/F♯   **Em7**
Ev - 'rything that we should be.

             Cadd9
I'll bet she's beautiful,   that girl he talks about.

G5   **D/F♯**
And she's got ev'rything that I have to live without.

G5   **Em7**   **Cadd9**
Drew talks ____ to me.

   D/F♯   **G5**
I laugh ____ 'cause it's just so funny

        Em7   **Cadd9** **D/F♯**
That I can't ____ even see ____ an - yone when he's with me.

Em7   **Cadd9**   **Csus2**
He says he's so in love,   he's fin'lly got it right.

G5   **D/F♯**
I wonder if he knows he's all I think about at night.

Chorus 1

G5   D/F♯
He's the reason for the teardrops on my guitar,

Em7   Cadd9
The only thing that keeps me wishing on a wishing star.

G5   D/F♯
He's the song in the car   I keep singing,

                    Em7   Cadd9 Csus2
Don't know why ____ I do.

Verse 2

G5   Em7   Cadd9
Drew walks ____ by me.

   D/F♯   G5
Can ____ he tell that I can't breathe?

                    Em7   Cadd9
And there he goes ____ so perfectly,

         D/F♯
The kind of flawless I wish I could be.

Em7   Cadd9   Csus2
She better hold him tight,   give him all her love,

G5   D/F♯
Look in those beautiful eyes ____ and know she's lucky 'cause

Chorus 2   *Repeat Chorus 1*

Guitar Solo | G5 | Em7 | Cadd9 | D/F# |

| | Em7   Cadd9 |
| **Pre-Chorus** | So I drive home alone.   As I turn out the light, |

G5   D/F#
I'll put his picture down and   maybe get some sleep tonight.

| | G5   D/F# |
| **Chorus 3**| 'Cause he's the reason for the teardrops on my guitar, |

Em7   Cadd9
The only one who's got e - nough of me to break my heart.

G5   D/F#   Em7
He's the song in the car   I keep singing, don't know why ___ I do.

Cadd9 Csus2   G5   D/F#
He's the time ___ taken up, but there's nev - er enough

            Em7   Cadd9 Csus2
And he's all ___ that I need to fall in - to.

| | G5   Em7   Cadd9 |
| **Outro** | Drew looks ___ at me, |

      D/F#   G
I fake ___ a smile so he won't see.

Tim McGraw

Words and Music by
Taylor Swift and Liz Rose

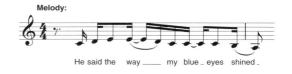

Melody:

He said the way ____ my blue _ eyes shined _

(Capo 5th fret)

G5   Em   C   D5   Dsus4   D   Em7   G/B   Cmaj7

Intro

| G | Em | C | D5 |

Verse 1

G5   Em
  He said the way my blue eyes shined

                          C
Put those Georgia stars to shame ____ that night.

               D5 Dsus4 D Dsus4
I said, "That's a lie."

G5   Em7
  Just a boy in it Chevy truck

                   C   Dsus4 D
That had a tendency of getting stuck on back roads at night.

Pre-Chorus 1

           C   D
And I was   right there beside him   all summer long.

Dsus4 C   G/B   C   D
  And then the time we woke up to find that   summer gone.

But when you think…

Chorus 1

G5   Em
Tim McGraw, I hope you think my fav'rite song,

        C
The one we danced to all night long,

      Dsus4   D
The moon like a spotlight on the lake.

      G5   Em
When you think happiness, I hope you think that little black dress,

      C   Dsus4   D
Think of my head on your chest and my old ___ faded blue jeans.

       C   D   G5
When you think Tim McGraw,   I hope you think of me.

Verse 2

G5   Em
 September saw a month of tears

           C   D
And thanking God that you weren't ___ here to see me like ___ that.

G5   Em7
 But in a box beneath my bed

       C   D5
Is a letter that you ___ never read from three summers back.

Pre-Chorus 2

C   D5
 It's hard not to find it all a little bittersweet.

    C   G/B   C   D
And looking back on all ___ of that, it's nice to believe

When you think...

Chorus 2 *Repeat Chorus 1*

Bridge

         C
And I'm back for the first time since then,

Dsus4   D
  I'm standing on your street.

          C   G/B
And there's a letter left on your ____ doorstep

          C   D
And the first thing that you'll read

Chorus 3

         G5   Em
Is when you think Tim McGraw, I hope you think my ____ fav'rite song.

               C
Someday you'll turn your radio on,

        Dsus4   D
I hope it takes ____ you back to that place.

      Dsus4   G5   Em
When you ____ think happiness, I hope you think that little black dress,

         C   Dsus4   D
Think of my head on your chest and my old ____ faded blue jeans.

      Dsus4 C   D   G5
When you think   Tim McGraw,   I hope you think of me.

           Em   C Cmaj7
Oh, think of me, ____ mm.

Outro

G5   Em7
  He said the way my blue eyes shined

                     C
Put those Georgia stars to shame ____ that night.

        D5 G5
I said, "That's a lie."

Tell Me Why

Words and Music by
Taylor Swift and Liz Rose

Melody:

I took a   chance, _

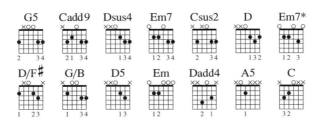

Intro
| G5 | | |

Verse 1

Cadd9   **G5**
I took a chance,   I took a shot.

Dsus4   **Em7**   **Cadd9**
And you might think I'm bulletproof, but I'm not.

                         G5
You took a swing,   I took it hard.

Dsus4   **Em7**
And down here from the ground I see who you are.

Chorus 1

  Csus2   **G5**
  I'm sick and tired of your attitude,

               D
I'm feeling like I don't know you.

            Em7*
You tell me that you love me, then cut me down.

Csus2   **G5**
  And I need you like a heartbeat,

              D
But you know you got a mean streak.

          Em7* **D/F♯**   **G5** **G/B** **Csus2**
Makes me run for cover when you're ___ a - round.

             D
And here's to you   and your temper.

      G5   **D/F♯**   **Em7***
Yes, I re - member what you said last night.

        Csus2   **D5**
And I know   that you see what you're do - ing to me.

D N.C.   **G5**
  Tell me why.

Verse 2

  Csus2 N.C.   **G5**
    You could write a book

    N.C.   **D**   **N.C.**   **Em**
On   how to ruin someone's   perfect day.

Csus2   **G5**
  Well, I get so con - fused and frustrated.

  D5   **Em**
For - get what I'm try'n' to say. ___ Oh, oh.

Chorus 2

Csus2   G5
  I'm sick and tired of your reasons,

                       D
I got no one to be - lieve in.

                    Em7*
You tell me that you want me, then push me around.

Csus2   G5
  And I need you like a heartbeat,

                      D
But you know you got a mean streak.

                 Em7* D/F♯   G5   G/B   Csus2
Makes me run for cover   when you're ___ a - round.

                  D
Here's to you ___ and your temper.

         G5   D/F♯   Em7*
Yes, I re - member what you said last night.

            Csus2   D
And I know   that you see what you're do - ing to me.

            G5
Tell me why.

Bridge

          D/F♯ Em   Csus2
Why _____ do you have to make me feel small

  G5   Dadd4
So you can feel whole inside?

Em   Csus2
Why do you have to put down my dreams

  A5   C   D5
So you're the only thing on my ___ mind?

Chorus 3

Cadd9   **G5**
  And I'm sick and tired of your attitude,

                 Dsus4
I'm feeling like I don't know you.

             Em7   **Csus2**
You tell me that you want me, and cut me down.

               G5
I'm sick and tired of your reasons,

            D
I got no one to be - lieve in.

           Em7* **D/F♯**   **G5**   **G/B** **Csus2**
You ask me for my love   then you push me around.

          D
Here's to you   and your temper.

      G5   **D/F♯**   **Em7***
Yes, I re - member what you said last night.

          Csus2   **D**
And I know   that you see what you're do - ing to me.

     G5   **Em7***   **Csus2** **D** **G/B**
Tell me ___ why. Why? Tell me why. ___ Oh.

Outro

Csus2   **G5**
  I take a step back,   let you go.

D   **Em**   **G5**
  I told you I'm not bulletproof, now you know.

Tied Together with a Smile

Words and Music by
Taylor Swift and Liz Rose

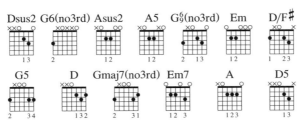

Intro | Dsus2   G6(no3rd) | Asus2 | Dsus2   G6(no3rd) | A5 |

| Dsus2   G⁶₉(no 3rd)
Verse 1   Seems the only one who doesn't see your beau - ty

| Dsus2   G⁶₉(no3rd)
Is the face in the mirror looking back at ____ you.

Dsus2   G⁶₉(no3rd)
You walk around here thinking you're not ____ pretty,

| Em D/F♯ G5   Em D/F♯ G5
But that's not true _____ 'cause I know you.

| D
Chorus 1   Hold on, baby, you're losin' it.

Gmaj7(no3rd)   Em7
The water's high, you're jumping into it and lettin' go

| A   D
And no one knows   that you cry,

| Gmaj7(no3rd)   Em7
But you don't tell anyone   that you might not be the golden one.

| D/F♯   G5
And you're tied to - gether with a smile,

| D A   Em7 D/F♯ G5
But you're comin' undone. ____ Oh, whoa, whoa.

Verse 2

      D5   **G5**
I guess it's true that love was all you want - ed

                  D5   **G5**
'Cause you're   giving it away like it's extra change.

D5   **G5**
Hoping it will end up in his pock - et,

      Em7   **D/F♯**   **G5**
But he leaves you out like a penny in the rain.

Em7   **D/F♯**   **G5**
Oh, 'cause it's not his price to pay, ____ it's not his price to pay.

Chorus 2   *Repeat Chorus 1*

    Dsus2
Chorus 3   Hold on, baby, you're losin' it.

G5   **Em**
The water's high, you're jumping into it and   lettin' go

   G5   **D**
And no one knows ____ that you cry,

                 Gmaj7(no3rd)   **Em7**
But you don't tell anyone   that you might not be the golden one.

      D/F♯   **G5**
And you're tied to - gether with a smile,

                   D A   **Em7**
But you're comin' undone. _____ Oh, whoa, whoa. ____ oh.

    D/F♯   **G5**   **D A**
You're tied to - gether with a smile, but you're comin' undone.

        Em7   **D/F♯**   **G5**
Oh, whoa, ____ whoa. Good - bye baby,   with a smile, baby, baby.

Outro |**D** |**A** |**Em7** **D/F♯**|**G5** |
            Oh. _____

            ‖:**D** |**A** |**Em7** **D/F♯**|**G5**   :‖ *Repeat and fade*

Today Was a Fairytale

from VALENTINE'S DAY

Words and Music by
Taylor Swift

Melody:

To-day was a fair-y-tale.

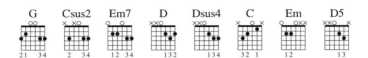

G   Csus2   Em7   D   Dsus4   C   Em   D5

Intro   ‖: G Csus2 | | Em7 D | Dsus4 :‖

Verse 1

G   Csus2   Em7
Today was a fairytale. You were the prince.

          D   Dsus4 G
I used to be a damsel in dis - tress.

          Csus2   Em7
You took me by the hand and you picked me up at six.

         D   Dsus4 G Csus2 Em7 D
Today was a fairytale.

        Dsus4   G   Csus2 Em7 D Dsus4
Today ____ was a fairytale.

Verse 2

G   Csus2
Today was a fairytale.

        Em7   D   Dsus4
I wore a dress, you wore a dark grey tee shirt.

G   Csus2   Em7
You told me I was pretty when I looked like a mess.

        D   Dsus4
Today was a fairytale.

Pre-Chorus 1

      C   Em   D5   C   D5
Time slows down   whenever you're a - round.

Chorus 1

G   Csus2   Em7
But can you feel this magic in the air?

           D   G
It must've been the way you kissed me.

    Csus2   Em7
Fell in love when I saw you standing there.

        D   G   Csus2
It must've been the way today was a fairytale.

Em7   D   G   Csus2 Em7 D
It must've been the way today was a fairytale.

Verse 3

G   Csus2
Today was a fairytale.

        Em7   D
You've got a smile takes me to another planet.

G   Csus2   Em7
Ev'ry move you make, ev'rything you say is right.

    D
Today was a fairytale.

G   Csus2
Today was a fairytale.

        Em7   D
All that I can say is now it's getting so much clearer.

G   Csus2   Em7
Nothing made sense 'till the time I saw your face.

    D
Today was a fairytale.

Pre-Chorus 2   *Repeat Pre-Chorus 1*

Chorus 2   *Repeat Chorus 1*

Interlude |G Csus2 | |Em7 D | Dsus4 |
|G Csus2 | |Em7 D | |

Pre-Chorus 3

   C   Em   D5
  Time slows down   whenever you're around.

   C   Em   D5   C
  I can feel my heart, it's beating in my chest.

             Em   D5   C   D5
  Did you feel it?   I can't put this down.

Chorus 3

   G   Csus2   Em7
‖:   But can you feel this magic in the air?

       D   Dsus4   G
  It must've been the way you kissed me.

   Csus2   Em7
  Fell in love when I saw you standing there.

       D   Dsus4   G   Csus2
  It must've been the way. :‖ Today was a fairytale.

 Em7   D   G   Csus2 Em7 D Dsus4
  It must've been the way today was a fairytale.

Outro

  G Csus2 Em7 D Dsus4
  Oh, _____ oh,

   G Csus2   Em7 D
  Yeah, _____ oh.

  Dsus4   G
  Today was a fairytale.

The Way I Loved You

Words and Music by
Taylor Swift and John Rich

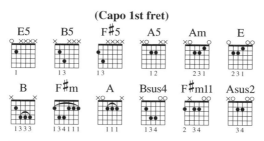

(Capo 1st fret)

Intro

| E5 | B5 | F#5 | A5 Am |
| E | B | F#m | A B |

Verse 1

E5   B5
He is sensible and so incredible

      F#5   A5
And all my single friends are jeal - ous.

E5   B5
He says ev'rything I need to hear

      F#5   A5
And it's like I couldn't ask for anything ___ better.

E5   B5
He opens up my door and I get into his car

      F#5   Am
And he ___ says, "You look beautiful tonight."

And I feel perfectly fine.

Chorus 1

E
But I miss screaming and fighting and kissing in the rain

Bsus4
And it's two a.m. and I'm cursing your name.

F#m11
You're so in love that you act insane.

Asus2   Bsus4
And that's the way I loved you.

E
  Breakin' down and coming undone,

Bsus4
It's a   roller coaster kinda rush.

F#m11
And I   never knew I could feel that much

Asus2   Am
And that's the way I loved you.

Interlude | E | B | F#m | A   B |

Verse 2

E5   B5
He respects my space and never makes me wait

F#5   A5
And he calls exactly when he says he will.

E5   B5
He's close to my mother, talks business with my father.

F#5   Am
He's charming and endearing and I'm comf'table.

Chorus 2   *Repeat Chorus 1*

Guitar Solo | E | Bsus4 | F#m11 | Asus2 |

Bridge

F#5   A
He can't see the smile I'm faking,

           E
And my heart's not breaking

            B5
'Cause I'm not feeling anything at all.

    F#5
And you were wild and crazy,

A   E
Just so frustrating, in - toxicating, complicated.

B5   Asus2
Got away by some mistake and now I miss

Chorus 3

E5
Screaming and fighting and kissing in the rain.

    B5
It's two a.m. and I'm cursing your name.

    F#5
I'm so in love that I acted insane.

     A   B
And that's the way I loved you.

E
  Breakin' down and coming undone,

    Bsus4
It's a   roller coaster kinda rush.

     F#m11
And I   never knew I could feel that much.

    Asus2   Bsus4
And that's the way I loved you.

Outro

E B   F#m
  Whoa, whoa, oh, ___ oh.

    A   B
Oh, and that's the way I loved you.

E   B   F#m
  Oh, oh, oh, oh, ___ oh, oh, oh, whoa.

Never knew I could feel that much,

    A   Am   E
And that's the way I loved you.

You Belong with Me

Words and Music by
Taylor Swift and Liz Rose

Tune down 1/2 step:
(low to high) E♭-A♭-D♭-G♭-B♭-E♭

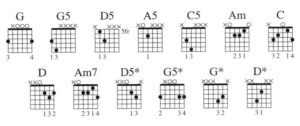

Intro

| N.C.(G) | | | |

Verse 1

G5   D5
You're on the phone with your girlfriend, she's upset.

              A5
She's going off about something that you said

           C5
'Cause she doesn't get your humor like I do.

G5   D5
I'm in the room, it's a typical Tuesday night.

              A5
I'm listening to the kind of music she doesn't like,

         C5
And she'll never know your story like I do.

Pre-Chorus 1
      Am   **C**
But she wears short skirts, I wear T-shirts.

G   **D**
She's cheer captain and I'm on the bleachers

Am7   **C**
Dreaming 'bout the day when you wake up and find

               D5*
That what you're   looking for has been here the whole time.

Chorus 1
               G5*
If you could see that I'm the one who understands you,

D
Been here all along.

               Am   **C**
So why can't you see, ee, you belong with me, ee?

               N.C.(G)
You belong with me.

Verse 2
G5   **D5**
Walk in the streets with you and your worn out jeans,

                       A5
I can't help thinking this is how it ought to be.

                       C5
Laughing on a park bench, thinking to myself,

"Hey, isn't this easy?"

G5   **D5**
And you've got a smile that could light up this whole town.

                        A5
I haven't seen it in a while since she brought you down.

You say you're fine, I know you better than that.

C5
  Hey, what are you doing with a girl like that?

Pre-Chorus 2

    Am   C
She wears high heels, I wear sneakers.

    G   D
She's cheer captain and I'm on the bleachers

    Am   C
Dreaming 'bout the day when you wake up and find

               D
That what you're   looking for has been here the whole time.

Chorus 2

        G5*
If you could see that I'm the one who understands you,

    D
Been here all along.

        Am   C
So why can't you see, ee, you belong with me, ee?

    G5*
Standing by, waiting at your back door.

    D
All this time how could you not know?

     Am   C
Ba - by, ee, you belong with me, ee.

You belong with me.

Guitar Solo

| G5* | | | D | | | |
| Am | | | C | | | |

                    Oh, I remember you

Bridge

    Am   **C**
Driving to my house in the middle of the night.

       G5*   **D**
I'm the one who makes you laugh when you know you're 'bout to cry.

    Am   **C**
I know your fav'rite songs and you tell me 'bout your dreams.

       G5*   **D5***
Think I know where you belong, think I know it's with me.

Chorus 3

       G*
Can't you see that I'm the one who understands you?

D*
Been here all along,

          Am   **C**
So why can't you see, ee, you belong with me, ee?

G5*
Standing by, waiting at your back door.

D
All this time how could you not know?

      Am   **C**
Ba - by, ee, you belong with me, ee.

            G5*
You belong with me.

Outro

           D
You belong with me.

                 Am
Have you ever thought just may - be, ee,

       C
You belong with me, ee?

      G5*
You belong with me.

You're Not Sorry

Words and Music by
Taylor Swift

Melody:

All this time I was wast-ing, hop-ing you would

Tune down 1/2 step:
(low to high) E♭-A♭-D♭-G♭-B♭-E♭

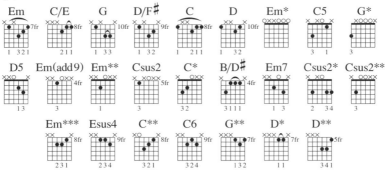

Em   C/E   G   D/F#   C   D   Em*   C5   G*

D5   Em(add9)   Em**   Csus2   C*   B/D#   Em7   Csus2*   Csus2**

Em***   Esus4   C**   C6   G**   D*   D**

Intro |Em C/E |G D/F# |Em C |G D/F# |

Verse 1

    Em   **C**   **G**
All this time I was wasting, hoping you would come around.

    D/F#   **Em**   **C**
    I've been giving out chances ev'ry time

                   G
And all you do is let __ me down.

    D/F#   **Em**   **C**   **G**
    And it's taken me this long, baby, but I figured you ____ out.

    D/F#   **Em**
    And you're thinking we'll be fine again,

        C   **G**
But not this time ____ around.

Chorus 1

      D   Em*   C5
You don't have to call any - more,

          G*   D5
I won't pick up the phone.

              Em(add9) Em** Csus2
This is the last   straw,

C*   G*   D5
  Don't wanna hurt anymore.

N.C.(B/D♯) Em7
And you can tell me that you're sorry,

   Csus2*   G*   D5
But I don't believe you, baby, like I did before.

          N.C.(B/D♯) Em(add9) Em**
You're not   sorry,

Csus2 Csus2** G*   D5   N.C.(Em) (C) (G) (D)
      No, no, _____ no, ____ no.

Verse 2

         Em   C   G
You're looking so innocent, I might believe you if I did - n't know.

D/F♯   Em
  Could-a loved you all my life

      C   G
If you hadn't left me waiting in ___ the cold.

D/F♯   Em
  And you got your share of secrets

         C   G   D/F♯
And I'm tired of being last ___ to know, whoa.

             Em
And now you're asking me to listen

      C   G
'Cause it worked each time ___ before.

Chorus 2

         D   **Em***   **C5**
But you don't have to call any - more,

          G*   **D5**
I won't pick up the phone.

         N.C.(B/D♯) **Em(add9)** **Em*** **Csus2**
This is ___ the   last   straw,

C*   **G***   **D5**
  Don't wanna hurt anymore.

          Em7
And you can tell me that you're sorry,

       Csus2*   **G***   **D5***
But I don't believe you, baby, like I did before.

        N.C.(B/D♯) **Em(add9)** **Em***
You're not   sorry,

      Csus2 **Csus2*** **G*** **D5**
No, no.

           Em*   **C5** **G*** **D5**
You're not sorry, no, no.

Guitar Solo   ‖: **Em*** **C5** │**G***   **D5** :‖

Verse 3

           Em**   **Esus4**
You had me crawling for you, honey,

       C**   **C6**   **G****   **D***
And it never would have gone away, ___ no.

          Em   **C****   **G****
You used to shine so bright, but I watched all of it fade.

Chorus 3

D**   Em*   C5
So you don't have to call any - more,

       G*   D5
I won't pick up the phone.

         N.C.(B/D♯)   Em(add9)   Em**   Csus2
This is ____ the   last   straw,

C*   G*   D5
  There's nothing left to beg for.

          Em(add9)   Em**
And you can tell me that you're sorry,

      Csus2   Csus2**   G*   D5*
But I don't believe you, baby, like I did before.

           Em(add9)   Em**   Csus2   Csus2**   G*   D5
You're not sorry,   no,   no.

         Em7   Csus2*   G*   D5
You're not sorry, no, no.

Outro

     Em*   C5   G*   D5
No, no, no, no, no, ____ no, no.

     Em*   C5   G* D5
No, no, no, no, no.

      Em*   C5 G*   D5
Whoa,   oh, oh. ____   Oh, oh, ____ oh.

Em*   C5   G*   D5
  Oh, oh, ____ oh, no, ____ no.

Em   C   G   D   Em   C   G   D   Em
     No, ____   no, ____ no.

White Horse

Words and Music by
Taylor Swift and Liz Rose

Melody:

Say you're sor - ry, that face ___

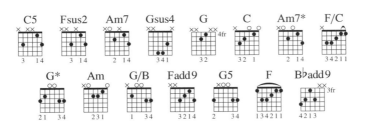

C5   Fsus2   Am7   Gsus4   G   C   Am7*   F/C

G*   Am   G/B   Fadd9   G5   F   Bbadd9

Intro   ‖:C5 |Fsus2 |Am7 |Fsus2   :‖

Verse 1

C5   Fsus2
  Say you're sorry, that face ____ of an angel

      Am7   Fsus2
Comes out ____ just when you need it to

C5   Fsus2
  As I paced back and forth ____ all this time

     Am7   Fsus2
'Cause I honestly believed in ____ you.

    Am7   Fsus2
Hold - ing on, the days ____ drag on.

      Gsus4   G
Stupid girl,   I should've known, I should've known

Chorus 1

                  C   Am7*
That I'm not a prin - cess, this ain't a fair - y tale.

            F/C   G*
I'm not the one ___ you'll sweep off her feet, lead her up the stairwell.

            C   Am7*
This ain't Hollywood, this is a small ___ town.

          F/C   G*
I was a dream - er before you went and let me down.

          Am   G/B
Now it's too ___ late for you

          Fadd9   C5
And your white ___ horse to come around.

Verse 2

C5   Fsus2
   Maybe I was naive,   got lost in your eyes

   Am7   Fadd9
And never really had a chance.

C5   Fsus2
   My mistake, I didn't know to be in love

        Am7   Fadd9
You had to fight to have the upper hand.

     Am7   F/C
I had so many dreams about you ___ and me.

     G5
Happy end - ings, now I know

Chorus 2

                  C   Am7*
That I'm not a prin - cess, this ain't a fair - y tale.

            F/C   G*
I'm not the one ___ you'll sweep off her feet, lead her up the stairwell.

            C   Am7*
This ain't Hollywood, this is a small ___ town.

          F/C   G*
I was a dream - er before you went and let me down.

          Am   G/B
Now it's too ___ late for you

          Fadd9   C Am7* F G5
And your white ___ horse to come around.

Bridge

Am   G/B   F/C
And there you are on your ____ knees,

C   G/B   F/C
Begging for for - giveness,   begging for me.

C   G/B   F/C   B♭add9
Just like I always wanted,   but I'm so sor - ry

Chorus 3

                    C   Am7*
'Cause I'm not your prin - cess, this ain't a fair - y tale.

                 F   G5
I'm gonna find ____ someone someday who might ac - tually treat me well.

          C   Am7*
This is a big world, that was a small ____ town

              F/C   G*
There in my rear ____ view mirror disappear - ing now.

            Am   G/B   Fadd9
And it's too ____ late for you ____ and your white ____ horse,

            Am   G/B
Now it's too ____ late for you

            Fadd9   C5
And your white ____ horse to catch me ____ now.

Fsus2   Am7*
Oh, whoa, ____ whoa, whoa.

Outro

F/C   C   F/C
Try and catch me now, ____ oh.

Am7*   F   C
It's too late   to catch me now.

Guitar Chord Songbooks

Each book includes complete lyrics, chord symbols, and guitar chord diagrams.

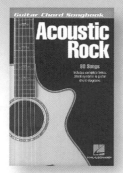
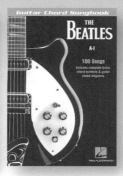
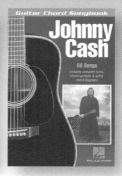
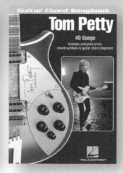

Acoustic Rock
80 acoustic favorites: Blackbird • Blowin' in the Wind • Layla • Maggie May • Me and Julio down by the Schoolyard • Pink Houses • and more.
00699540..................................$17.95

Alabama
50 of Alabama's best: Born Country • Dixieland Delight • Feels So Right • Mountain Music • Song of the South • Why Lady Why • and more.
00699914 ....$14.95

The Beach Boys
59 favorites: California Girls • Don't Worry Baby • Fun, Fun, Fun • Good Vibrations • Help Me Rhonda • Wouldn't It Be Nice • dozens more!
00699566..................................$14.95

The Beatles (A-I)
An awesome reference of Beatles hits: All You Need Is Love • The Ballad of John and Yoko • Get Back • Good Day Sunshine • A Hard Day's Night • Hey Jude • I Saw Her Standing There • and more!
00699558..................................$17.99

The Beatles (J-Y)
100 more Beatles hits: Lady Madonna • Let It Be • Ob-La-Di, Ob-La-Da • Paperback Writer • Revolution • Twist and Shout • When I'm Sixty-Four • and more.
00699562..................................$17.99

Blues
80 blues tunes: Big Boss Man • Cross Road Blues (Crossroads) • Damn Right, I've Got the Blues • Pride and Joy • Route 66 • Sweet Home Chicago • and more.
00699733 ....$12.95

Broadway
80 stage hits: All I Ask of You • Bali Ha'i • Edelweiss • Hello, Dolly! • Memory • Ol' Man River • People • Seasons of Love • Sunrise, Sunset • and more.
00699920 ....$14.99

Johnny Cash
58 Cash classics: A Boy Named Sue • Cry, Cry, Cry • Daddy Sang Bass • Folsom Prison Blues • I Walk the Line • RIng of Fire • Solitary Man • and more.
00699648..................................$17.99

Steven Curtis Chapman
65 from this CCM superstar: Be Still and Know • Cinderella • For the Sake of the Call • Live Out Loud • Speechless • With Hope • and more.
00700702 ....$17.99

Children's Songs
70 songs for kids: Alphabet Song • Bingo • The Candy Man • Eensy Weensy Spider • Puff the Magic Dragon • Twinkle, Twinkle Little Star • and more!
00699539..................................$16.99

Christmas Carols
80 Christmas carols: Angels We Have Heard on High • The Holly and the Ivy • I Saw Three Ships • Joy to the World • O Holy Night • Silent Night • What Child Is This? • and more.
00699536..................................$12.95

Christmas Songs
80 Christmas favorites: The Christmas Song • Feliz Navidad • Jingle-Bell Rock • Merry Christmas, Darling • Rudolph the Red-Nosed Reindeer • more.
00699537..................................$12.95

Eric Clapton
75 of Slowhand's finest: I Shot the Sheriff • Knockin' on Heaven's Door • Layla • Strange Brew • Tears in Heaven • Wonderful Tonight • and more!
00699567..................................$15.99

Classic Rock
80 rock essentials: Beast of Burden • Cat Scratch Fever • Hot Blooded • Money • Rhiannon • Sweet Emotion • Walk on the Wild Side • more
00699598..................................$15.99

Country
80 country standards: Boot Scootin' Boogie • Crazy • Hey, Good Lookin'• Sixteen Tons • Through the Years • Your Cheatin' Heart • more.
00699534..................................$14.95

Country Favorites
Over 60 songs: Achy Breaky Heart (Don't Tell My Heart) • Brand New Man • Gone Country • The Long Black Veil • Make the World Go Away • and more.
00700609 ....$14.99

Country Standards
60 songs: By the Time I Get to Phoenix • El Paso • The Gambler • I Fall to Pieces • Jolene • King of the Road • Put Your Hand in the Hand • A Rainy Night in Georgia • more.
00700608 ....$12.95

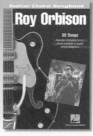

Cowboy Songs

Over 60 tunes: Back in the Saddle Again • Happy Trails • Home on the Range • Streets of Laredo • The Yellow Rose of Texas • and more.
00699636...................................$12.95

Crosby, Stills & Nash

37 hits: Chicago • Dark Star • Deja Vu • Marrakesh Express • Our House • Southern Cross • Suite: Judy Blue Eyes • Teach Your Children • and more.
00701609................................. $12.99

Neil Diamond

50 songs: America • Cherry, Cherry • Cracklin' Rosie • Forever in Blue Jeans • I Am...I Said • Love on the Rocks • Song Sung Blue • Sweet Caroline • and dozens more!
00700606 ....$14.99

Disney

56 super Disney songs: Be Our Guest • Friend like Me • Hakuna Matata • It's a Small World • Under the Sea • A Whole New World • Zip-A-Dee-Doo-Dah • and more!
00701071 ....$14.99

The Doors

60 classics: Break on Through to the Other Side • The End • L.A. Woman • Light My Fire • Love Her Madly • Love Me Two Times • People Are Strange • Riders on the Storm • Twentieth Century Fox • and more.
00699888 ....$15.99

Early Rock

80 early rock classics: All I Have to Do Is Dream • Fever • He's So Fine • I'm Sorry • Lollipop • Puppy Love • Sh-Boom (Life Could Be a Dream) • and more.
00699916 ....$14.99

Folk Pop Rock

80 songs: American Pie • Dust in the Wind • Me and Bobby McGee • Somebody to Love • Time in a Bottle • and more.
00699651...........................$14.95

Folksongs

80 folk favorites: Aura Lee • Camptown Races • Danny Boy • Man of Constant Sorrow • Nobody Knows the Trouble I've Seen • When the Saints Go Marching In • and more.
00699541...............................$12.95

Gospel Hymns

80 hymns: Amazing Grace • Give Me That Old Time Religion • I Love to Tell the Story • The Old Rugged Cross • Shall We Gather at the River? • Wondrous Love • and more.
00700463 ....$14.99

Grand Ole Opry®

80 great songs: Abilene • Act Naturally • Country Boy • Crazy • Friends in Low Places • He Stopped Loving Her Today • Wings of a Dove • dozens more!
00699885 ....$16.95

Hillsong United

65 top worship songs: Break Free • Everyday • From the Inside Out • God Is Great • Look to You • Now That You're Near • Salvation Is Here • To the Ends of the Earth • and more.
00700222 ....$12.95

Irish Songs

45 Irish favorites: Danny Boy • Girl I Left Behind Me • Harrigan • I'll Tell Me Ma • The Irish Rover • My Wild Irish Rose • When Irish Eyes Are Smiling • and more!
00701044 ....$14.99

Jazz Standards

50 songs: Ain't Misbehavin' • Cheek to Cheek • In the Wee Small Hours of the Morning • The Nearness of You • Stardust • The Way You Look Tonight • and more.
00700972 ....$14.99

Billy Joel

60 Billy Joel favorites: • It's Still Rock and Roll to Me • The Longest Time • Piano Man • She's Always a Woman • Uptown Girl • We Didn't Start the Fire • You May Be Right • and more.
00699632...................................$15.99

Elton John

60 songs: Bennie and the Jets • Candle in the Wind • Crocodile Rock • Goodbye Yellow Brick Road • Pinball Wizard • Sad Songs (Say So Much) • Tiny Dancer • Your Song • and more.
00699732 ....$15.99

Latin Songs

60 favorites: Bésame Mucho (Kiss Me Much) • The Girl from Ipanema (Garôta De Ipanema) • The Look of Love • So Nice (Summer Samba) • and more.
00700973 ....$14.99

Love Songs

65 romantic ditties: Baby, I'm-A Want You • Fields of Gold • Here, There and Everywhere • Let's Stay Together • Never My Love • The Way We Were • more!
00701043...............................$14.99

Bob Marley

36 songs: Buffalo Soldier • Get up Stand Up • I Shot the Sheriff • Is This Love • Jamming • No Woman No Cry • One Love • Redemption Song • Stir It Up • and more.
00701704...............................$12.99

Paul McCartney

60 from Sir Paul: Band on the Run • Jet • Let 'Em In • Maybe I'm Amazed • No More Lonely Nights • Say Say Say • Take It Away • With a Little Luck • more!
00385035 ....$16.95

Steve Miller

33 hits: Dance Dance Dance • Jet Airliner • The Joker • Jungle Love • Rock'n Me • Serenade from the Stars • Swingtown • Take the Money and Run • and more.
00701146...............................$12.99

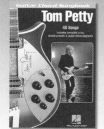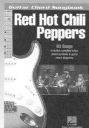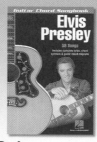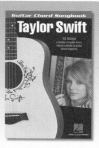

Motown

60 Motown masterpieces: ABC • Baby I Need Your Lovin' • I'll Be There • Just My Imagination • Lady Marmalade • Stop! In the Name of Love • You Can't Hurry Love • more.
00699734 ....$16.95

The 1950s

80 early rock favorites: High Hopes • Mister Sandman • Only You (And You Alone) • Put Your Head on My Shoulder • Que Sera, Sera (Whatever Will Be, Will Be) • Tammy • That's Amoré • and more.
00699922 ....$14.99

The 1980s

80 hits: Centerfold • Come on Eileen • Don't Worry, Be Happy • Got My Mind Set on You • Sailing • Should I Stay or Should I Go • Sweet Dreams (Are Made of This) • more.
00700551 ....$16.99

Nirvana

40 songs: About a Girl • Come as You Are • Heart Shaped Box • The Man Who Sold the World • Smells like Teen Spirit • You Know You're Right • and more.
00699762 ....$16.99

Roy Orbison

38 songs: Blue Bayou • Crying • Oh, Pretty Woman • Only the Lonely (Know the Way I Feel) • Pretty Paper • Running Scared • Working for the Man • You Got It • and more.
00699752 ....$12.95

Tom Petty

American Girl • Breakdown • Don't Do Me like That • Free Fallin' • Here Comes My Girl • Into the Great Wide Open • Mary Jane's Last Dance • Refugee • Runnin' Down a Dream • The Waiting • more.
00699883 ....$15.99

Pop/Rock

80 chart hits: Against All Odds • Come Sail Away • Every Breath You Take • Hurts So Good • Kokomo • More Than Words • Smooth • Summer of '69 • and more.
00699538................................$14.95

Praise and Worship

80 favorites: Agnus Dei • He Is Exalted • I Could Sing of Your Love Forever • Lord, I Lift Your Name on High • More Precious Than Silver • Open the Eyes of My Heart • Shine, Jesus, Shine • and more.
00699634 ....$14.99

Elvis Presley

60 hits: All Shook Up • Blue Suede Shoes • Can't Help Falling in Love • Heartbreak Hotel • Hound Dog • Jailhouse Rock • Suspicious Minds • Viva Las Vegas • more.
00699633................................$14.95

Red Hot Chili Peppers

50 hits: Breaking the Girl • By the Way • Californication • Give It Away • Higher Ground • Love Rollercoaster • Scar Tissue • Suck My Kiss • Under the Bridge • What It Is • and more.
00699710................................$16.95

Rock Ballads

54 songs: Amanda • Boston • Brick • Landslide • Love Hurts • Mama, I'm Coming Home • She Will Be Loved • Waiting for a Girl like You • and more.
00701034 ....$14.99

Rock 'n' Roll

80 rock 'n' roll classics: At the Hop • Great Balls of Fire • It's My Party • La Bamba • My Boyfriend's Back • Peggy Sue • Stand by Me • more.
00699535................................$14.95

Bob Seger

41 favorites: Against the Wind • Hollywood Nights • Katmandu • Like a Rock • Night Moves • Old Time Rock & Roll • You'll Accomp'ny Me • and more!
00701147................................$12.99

Sting

50 favorites from Sting and the Police: Brand New Day • Can't Stand Losing You • Don't Stand So Close to Me • Every Breath You Take • Fields of Gold • King of Pain • Message in a Bottle • Roxanne • more.
00699921 ....$14.99

Taylor Swift

27 tunes: Fifteen • Hey Stephen • Love Story • Our Song • Picture to Burn • Tim McGraw • Today Was a Fairytale • White Horse • You Belong with Me • and more.
00701799................................$14.99

Three Chord Songs

65 includes: All Right Now • La Bamba • Lay Down Sally • Mony, Mony • Rock Around the Clock • Rock This Town • Werewolves of London • You Are My Sunshine • and more.
00699720 ....$12.95

Wedding Songs

50 songs that every gigging musician should know, including: Ave Maria • Butterfly Kisses • Endless Love • Have I Told You Lately • Longer • The Lord's Prayer • Sunrise, Sunset • Through the Years • and more.
00701005 ....$14.99

Hank Williams

68 classics: Cold, Cold Heart • Hey, Good Lookin' • Honky Tonk Blues • I'm a Long Gone Daddy • Jambalaya (On the Bayou) • Your Cheatin' Heart • and more.
00700607 ....$14.99

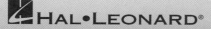

Complete contents listings available online at www.halleonard.com

Prices, contents and availability subject to change without notice.

HAL•LEONARD GUITAR PLAY-ALONG

This series will help you play your favorite songs quickly and easily. Just follow the tab and listen to the CD to hear how the guitar should sound, and then play along using th separate backing tracks. Mac or PC users can also slow down t tempo without changing pitch by using the CD in their compute The melody and lyrics are included in the book so that you ca sing or simply follow along.

1. ROCK
00699570 ....$16.99

2. ACOUSTIC
00699569 ....$16.95

3. HARD ROCK
00699573 ....$16.95

4. POP/ROCK
00699571 ....$16.99

5. MODERN ROCK
00699574 ....$16.99

6. '90s ROCK
00699572 ....$16.99

7. BLUES
00699575 ....$16.95

8. ROCK
00699585 ....$14.99

9. PUNK ROCK
00699576 ....$14.95

10. ACOUSTIC
00699586 ....$16.95

11. EARLY ROCK
0699579 ....$14.95

12. POP/ROCK
00699587 ....$14.95

13. FOLK ROCK
00699581 ....$14.95

14. BLUES ROCK
00699582 ....$16.95

15. R&B
00699583 ....$14.95

16. JAZZ
00699584 ....$15.95

17. COUNTRY
00699588 ....$15.95

18. ACOUSTIC ROCK
00699577 ....$15.95

19. SOUL
00699578 ....$14.95

20. ROCKABILLY
00699580 ....$14.95

21. YULETIDE
00699602 ....$14.95

22. CHRISTMAS
00699600 ....$15.95

23. SURF
00699635 ....$14.95

24. ERIC CLAPTON
00699649 ....$17.99

25. LENNON & McCARTNEY
00699642 ....$16.

26. ELVIS PRESLEY
00699643 ....$14.

27. DAVID LEE ROTH
00699645 ....$16.

28. GREG KOCH
00699646 ....$14.

29. BOB SEGER
00699647 ....$14.

30. KISS
00699644 ....$16.

31. CHRISTMAS HITS
00699652 ....$14.

32. THE OFFSPRING
00699653 ....$14.

33. ACOUSTIC CLASSICS
00699656 ....$16.

34. CLASSIC ROCK
00699658 ....$16.

35. HAIR METAL
00699660 ....$16.

36. SOUTHERN ROCK
00699661 ....$16.

86. BOSTON
00700465 ....$16.99

87. ACOUSTIC WOMEN
00700763 ....$14.99

88. GRUNGE
00700467 ....$16.99

91. BLUES INSTRUMENTALS
00700505 ....$14.99

92. EARLY ROCK INSTRUMENTALS
00700506 ....$12.99

93. ROCK INSTRUMENTALS
00700507 ....$16.99

96. THIRD DAY
00700560.................................$14.95

97. ROCK BAND
00700703.................................$14.99

98. ROCK BAND
00700704.................................$14.95

99. ZZ TOP
00700762 ....$16.99

100. B.B. KING
00700466 ....$14.99

102. CLASSIC PUNK
00700769.................................$14.99

103. SWITCHFOOT
00700773 ....$16.99

104. DUANE ALLMAN
00700846.................................$16.99

106. WEEZER
00700958 ....$14.99

108. THE WHO
00701053 ....$16.99

107. CREAM
00701069.................................$16.99

109. STEVE MILLER
00701054 ....$14.99

111. JOHN MELLENCAMP
00701056 ....$14.99

113. JIM CROCE
00701058 ....$14.99

114. BON JOVI
00701060 ....$14.99

115. JOHNNY CASH
00701070 ....$16.99

116. THE VENTURES
00701124 ....$14.99

119. AC/DC CLASSICS
00701356 ....$17.99

120. PROGRESSIVE ROCK
00701457.................................$14.99

122. CROSBY, STILLS & NASH
00701610.................................$16.99

123. LENNON & MCCARTNEY ACOUSTIC
00701614.................................$16.99

124. MODERN WORSHIP
00701629.................................$14.99

126. BOB MARLEY
00701701.................................$16.99

127. 1970s ROCK
00701739.................................$14.99

128. 1960s ROCK
00701740.................................$14.99

129. MEGADETH
00701741.................................$14.99

130. IRON MAIDEN
00701742 ....$14.99

131. 1990s ROCK
00701743.................................$14.99

133. TAYLOR SWIFT
00701894.................................$16.99

Prices, contents, and availability subject to change without notice.

FOR MORE INFORMATION,
SEE YOUR LOCAL MUSIC DEALER,
OR WRITE TO:

HAL•LEONARD®
CORPORATION
7777 W. BLUEMOUND RD. P.O. BOX 13819
MILWAUKEE, WISCONSIN 53213

For audio samples and complete songlists, visit Hal Leonard online at www.halleonard.com